30 Day Mediterranean Diet Challenge

30 Day Mediterranean Diet Challenge

Mediterranean Diet Cookbook 30 Day Meal Plan For Weight Loss and Optimal Health

By: Anna Ambrosia

30 Day Mediterranean Diet Challenge

Legal notice

This book is copyright (c) 2017 by Anna Ambrosia. All rights are reserved. This book may not be duplicated or copied, either in whole or in part, via any means including any electronic form of duplication such as recording or transcription. The contents of this book may not be transmitted, stored in any retrieval system, or copied in any other manner regardless of whether use is public or private without express prior permission of the publisher.

This book provides information only. The author does not offer any specific advice, including medical advice, nor does the author suggest the reader or any other person engage in any particular course of conduct in any specific situation. This book is not intended to be used as a substitute for any professional advice, medical or of any other variety. The reader accepts sole responsibility for how he or she uses the information contained in this book. Under no circumstances will the publisher or the author be held liable for damages of any kind arising either directly or indirectly from any information contained in this book.

30 Day Mediterranean Diet Challenge

Table of Contents

Introduction 10
Mediterranean Diet: The General Overview 12
Mediterranean Diet: A Path to Weight Loss and a Healthier Life 14
The Mediterranean Diet: What Foods to Eat and to Avoid 16
Day 1 22
Apple Oats Porridge 22
Avocado Tuna Salads 24
Simple Mixed Veggie 26
Day 2 28
Spinach Scrambled Egg with Tomato 28
Veggie Mushroom in Cabbage Leaves 30
Lemon Grass Fish Fritter 32
Day 3 34
Quinoa Salad Bowl 34
Macaroni Tuna Salads 36
Scrumptious Tuna Tomato 38
Day 4 40
Nutritious Tuna Sandwich 40
Cabbage Rolls in Brown Gravy 42
Cheesy Tomato Bowls 44
Day 5 46
Easy Paprika Omelet 46
Veggie Roll with Avocado 48
Hot Shrimps Black Pepper 50
Day 6 52
Almond Overnight Oats 52
Beautiful Mixed Salads 54
Potato Lentils Stew 55
Day 7 57
Original Banana Pancake 57
Zucchini Spaghetti Black Pepper 59

30 Day Mediterranean Diet Challenge

Veggie Mixed Quinoa 61
Day 8 63
Potato Hash Black Pepper 63
Summer Veggie Roll 65
Spiced Chicken Satay 67
Day 9 69
Olive Veggie Frittata 69
3 Minutes Broccoli Garlic 71
The Pumpkin Pot 73
Day 10 75
Minty Avocado Greenies 75
Tomato Green Peas Pizza 77
Quick Chickpeas Curry 79
Day 11 81
Banana and Dates Oat Porridge 81
Avocado Chickpeas Curry Salads 83
Delicious Chicken in Tomato Sauce 86
Day 12 88
Coconut Blueberry Scones 88
Fruity Beans Salads 90
Beef Meat Balls in Red Gravy 92
Day 13 94
Fresh Blueberry Dorayaki 94
Spicy Vegetable Curry in Blanket 96
Scrumptious Spinach Balls 99
Day 14 101
Cheese Tomato Sandwich 101
Mediterranean Lentils Black Pepper 103
Spicy Spaghetti Veggie 105
Day 15 107
Pineapple and Tomato Quinoa 107
Baked Potato Patties 109
Warm Zucchini Soup 111
Day 16 113
Egg Creamy Salad with Avocado 113

Energetic Kale Carrots with Chili 115
Broccoli Quinoa Casserole 117
Day 17 119
Apple Coconut Oatmeal 119
Orange Green Salads 121
Chicken in Curry Gravy 123
Day 18 125
Turkey Sandwich in Garlic 125
Cheesy Spinach Mushroom 127
Spicy Eggplant Stew 129
Day 19 131
Cheesy Asparagus Frittata 131
Tamarind Cabbage Stew 133
Shrimps Satay Sweet Honey 135
Day 20 137
Red Apple Pancake 137
Avocado Salads with Chicken and Mushroom 140
Quinoa Chickpea Curry 142
Day 21 144
Cinnamon Simple Oatmeal 144
Sautéed Green Spinach 146
Warm Lamb Skewers 148
Day 22 149
Nutritious Veggie Sandwich 149
Spicy Tropical Salads 152
Original Baked Chicken Wings 154
Day 23 156
Healthy Baked Beans on Toast 156
Avocado Lentils Salads 159
Special Curry Pasta 160
Day 24 162
Baked Sweet Potato with Cinnamon 162
Special Raw Fruits 164
Chicken Tomato Soup 166
Day 25 168

30 Day Mediterranean Diet Challenge

Sweet Apple Frittata 168
Hot Salmon Cakes 170
Tasty Lentils Soup.. 172
Day 26.. 174
Savory Oatmeal Breakfast 174
Vegetable Tortilla Roll 176
Mushroom Kabobs Black Pepper............................ 178
Day 27.. 179
Whole-Wheat Poffertjes with Cinnamon 179
Sautéed Chicken in Wrap... 182
Quinoa Bowl with Cucumber and Kale 184
Day 28.. 186
Lemon Scones with Almond 186
Creamy Cheesy Pasta.. 188
Appetizing Cauliflower Rice 190
Day 29.. 192
Overnight Almond Raisin Oatmeal......................... 192
Refreshing Fruits Bowl 194
Potato White Beans Soup... 196
Day 30.. 198
Thick Omelet in Tomato Gravy................................ 198
Spinach Pizza Tomato 200
Stuffed Tomatoes with Couscous............................ 202
Conclusion .... **Error! Bookmark not defined.**

Introduction

There is no denying that everyone wants to live longer, healthier lives with a good physical condition and ideal body weight. Having perfect health allows for more opportunities to spend quality time with the people we love, and it's even better to be able to enjoy these beautiful moments knowing that we look good. Unfortunately, leading a healthy life in this era is not so easy. Besides living in a polluted environment, having bad eating habits is the main reason that people tend to be so unhealthy. Being so busy and having limited time forces people to eat many kinds of unhealthy foods, seeing as they are cheap, convenient, and also tasty. Even though these foods have known adverse effects such as obesity and other deadly conditions, people continue to eat them. Potentially lethal diseases like cancer, type 2 diabetes, heart disease, high blood pressure, and many others have become the most feared ailments that suddenly take the beautiful moments in life away from us. It is all too often that we hear about a friend who is struggling with cancer or a relative that has passed away because of a heart attack. This can often come as a shock if these people are still young and productive. How can this happen to them? Again, junk food and unhealthy foods are a major factor, as they cause obesity and other health conditions. Not only does being overweight give an unappealing appearance, but it can also open the gate to a variety of serious illness. The excessive fat raises cholesterol and sugar levels, causes breathing problems, and increases the risk of mental illness.

So although it sounds unpleasant, people should leave all unhealthy food behind if living healthier is the goal. A healthier body, ideal weight, and overall higher quality of life are more attainable than you think by simply choosing an effective dieting method.

This book provides a brief explanation of the Mediterranean diet, which is a healthy dieting method that will help you to achieve a better health condition and lose weight at the same time. Complete with a meal plan for 30 days—including breakfast, lunch, and dinner—this book will be a great reference when applying the Mediterranean diet.

Mediterranean Diet: The General Overview

The Mediterranean diet is one of healthiest diets in the world and is often correlated with heart health and longevity. Being known as a healthy and effective way of controlling weight and decreasing the risk of a number of chronic illnesses, the Mediterranean diet is a dieting method that adopts the eating habits of the people who live in the countries that border the Mediterranean Sea.

The food consumed in the Mediterranean diet varies greatly, as there are lots of different countries around the Mediterranean Sea. The cuisines of the Middle East are different from those of Northern Italy and Southern Greece. However, all of the countries in the Mediterranean have a certain similar characteristic of eating, which include a high consumption of plant-based foods and a low intake of animal-based foods. There is the exception of fish, however, which the Mediterranean diet recommends you eat as your main source of protein.

The Mediterranean diet has a special, modified food pyramid that outlines how much of which foods people should eat, making it a trusted and effective dieting method. The principles of the Mediterranean diet according to the modified food pyramid are as follows:

- Eat lots of plant-based food such as vegetables and fruits each day.
- Choose whole grains (quinoa, brown rice, whole wheat bread, and bulgur) as your

- carbohydrate source instead of refined carbs.
- Eat fish and seafood several times per week, ideally at least twice a week.
- Poultry, eggs, and dairy should be eaten in moderation.
- Limit your consumption of red meat.
- Include nuts, lentils, and beans in your weekly meal plan.
- Always use olive oil as a substitute for butter or lard.
- You should drink lots of water and avoid alcohol, although wine is permitted in small amounts; a glass of wine each day is allowed for women, while men may have two glasses of wine per day.

Mediterranean Diet: A Path to Weight Loss and a Healthier Life

Even though the Mediterranean diet is an effective dieting method, it doesn't magically lead you to a significant amount of weight loss and a better physical condition within a short period of time. The Mediterranean diet is rather like a collection of healthy eating habits that will help you to reach your weight loss goals while still enjoying delicious food.

Instead of torturing yourself with a list of prohibited foods or hardly eating at all, the Mediterranean diet recommends that you focus on balancing your food choices, controlling your portions, managing your calorie intake, and increasing your physical exercise.

Placing emphasis on your food choices, the Mediterranean diet recommends that you consume any food that is low in fat and cholesterol, but high in protein and fiber. The best way to decrease your calorie intake is by reducing your consumption of fat, since fat contains more calories than carbohydrates and protein. Furthermore, by consuming lots of lean protein and fiber, your stomach will stay full longer and thus eliminate your food cravings. Another important factor in achieving weight loss is monitoring your calorie intake. If you want to reduce your weight, you must consume fewer calories than you burn. However, you don't need to be a professional nutritionist to lower your calorie intake. In order to lose a steady amount of weight, you simply need to reduce the portion sizes that you usually have and get more physical exercise. It's that easy! The Mediterranean diet is not only helps you lose weight, but it also improves your overall physical condition. The Mediterranean diet encourages you to live a better lifestyle by eating healthy food in proper portions and getting more physical exercise.

The Mediterranean Diet: What Foods to Eat and to Avoid

Listed below are the foods that are recommended in the Mediterranean diet:

- Fresh vegetables

Brussels sprouts
Broccoli
Kale
Onions
Tomatoes
Carrots
Cauliflower
Cucumbers
Spinach

- Fresh fruits

Bananas
Oranges
Apples
Dates
Grapes
Strawberries
Melons
Figs
Pears

- Legumes

Peas
Peanuts

Beans
Lentils
Chickpeas

- Whole grains

Whole oats
Whole grain pasta
Whole grain bread
Brown rice
Barley
Rye
Buckwheat

- Seeds and Nuts

Walnuts
Almonds
Cashews
Hazelnuts
Pumpkin seeds
Sunflower seeds

- Spices and herbs

Basil
Garlic
Rosemary
Nutmeg
Sage
Mint
Pepper
Cinnamon

30 Day Mediterranean Diet Challenge

- Root vegetables

Sweet potatoes
Turnips
Potatoes

- Poultry

Chicken
Turkey
Duck

- Seafood and fish

Sardines
Salmon
Tuna
Trout
Oysters
Shrimp
Mussels
Crab

- Eggs

Quail eggs
Chicken eggs
Duck eggs

- Dairy

Yogurt (especially Greek yogurt)
Cheese

- Healthy Fats

Olive oil
Avocado oil

Listed below are the foods to avoid in the Mediterranean diet:

- Added Sugar

Candy
Soda
Ice cream

- Refined grains

Pasta from refined grain
White bread

- Trans fats

Margarine
Butter
- Refined Oils

Canola oil
Cottonseed oil

- Processed food

Processed hot dogs
Processed sausages
Anything labeled "low-fat"

30 Day Mediterranean Diet Challenge

Day 1

Breakfast : Apple Oats Porridge

Lunch : Avocado Tuna Salads

Dinner : Simple Mixed Veggie

Apple Oats Porridge

Serving: 2

Nutrition Facts
Servings: 2
Per Serving
Calories 136
Total Fat 1.5g
Saturated Fat 0.2g
Trans Fat 0g
Cholesterol 0mg
Sodium 9mg
Potassium 197mg
Total Carb 29.5g
Dietary Fiber 4.9g
Sugars 11.8g
Protein 3g
Nutrition Facts
Servings: 2
Per Serving
Calories 136

Ingredients:

2 cups water

½ cup oatmeal

1 fresh green apple

¼ teaspoon cinnamon

Directions:

- Peel and cut the apple into slices then set aside.
- Pour water in a saucepan then bring to boil.
- Once it is boiled, stir in oatmeal over the boiling water. Stir until combined.
- Reduce the heat then bring to a simmer for about 15 minutes.
- After that, add sliced apple into the saucepan and sprinkle cinnamon on top.
- Stir for a few seconds then transfer the oats porridge to a serving bowl.
- Serve and enjoy warm

Avocado Tuna Salads

Serving: 4

Nutrition Facts
Servings: 4
Per Serving
Calories 221
Total Fat 13.6g
Saturated Fat 3.9g
Trans Fat 0g
Cholesterol 12mg
Sodium 48mg
Potassium 468mg
Total Carb 8.7g
Dietary Fiber 3.5g
Sugars 4.4g
Protein 17g
Nutrition Facts
Servings: 4
Per Serving
Calories 221

Ingredients:

½ cup cooked tuna

2 tablespoons Greek yogurt

¼ cup chopped cabbage

1 ripe avocado

¼ teaspoon pepper

Directions:

- Cut the avocado into halves then remove the flesh out.
- Cut the avocado into small cubes then place in a bowl and chill in the refrigerator.

- Next, place the chopped cabbage in a steamer over medium heat then steam for about 3 minutes until the cabbage is tender.
- Transfer the cabbage to the avocado bowl then pour Greek yogurt over the salads.
- Season with pepper then using 2 forks mix the salads until well combined.
- Enjoy immediately or chill in the refrigerator if you want to enjoy it later.

30 Day Mediterranean Diet Challenge

Simple Mixed Veggie

Serving: 1

Nutrition Facts
Servings: 1
Per Serving
Calories 70
Total Fat 1.3g
Saturated Fat 0.2g
Trans Fat 0g
Cholesterol 0mg
Sodium 62mg
Potassium 443mg
Total Carb 13.9g
Dietary Fiber 4.3g
Sugars 6.3g
Protein 2.3g
Nutrition Facts
Servings: 1
Per Serving
Calories 70

Ingredients:

½ cup chopped cabbage

½ cup shredded carrot

½ cup chopped cauliflower

2 tablespoons chopped leek

¼ teaspoon olive oil

2 tablespoons chopped onion

¼ teaspoon pepper

Directions:

- Preheat a skillet over medium heat then pours olive oil into it.
- Once it is hot, stir in chopped onion then sautés until wilted and aromatic.
- Next, add chopped all of the vegetables into the skillet then season with pepper. Stir well until the vegetable is wilted and completely cooked.
- After that, transfer the sautéed vegetables to a serving dish then enjoy.

Day 2

Breakfast : Spinach Scrambled Egg with Tomato
Lunch : Veggie Mushroom in Cabbage Leaves
Dinner : Lemon Grass Fish Fritter

Spinach Scrambled Egg with Tomato

Serving: 1

Nutrition Facts
Servings: 1
Per Serving
Calories 150
Total Fat 11.7g
Saturated Fat 2.4g
Trans Fat 0g
Cholesterol 164mg
Sodium 80mg
Potassium 441mg
Total Carb 6g
Dietary Fiber 2g
Sugars 3.6g
Protein 7.1g
Nutrition Facts
Servings: 1
Per Serving
Calories 150

Ingredients:

1 ½ teaspoons olive oil

½ cup chopped spinach

1 organic egg

¼ teaspoon pepper

1 medium red tomato, for garnish

Directions:

- Preheat a frying pan over medium heat then pour olive oil into it.
- Once it is hot, stir in spinach and sauté until wilted.
- Crack the egg then place in a bowl. Using a fork, stir vigorously until beaten.
- Pour the egg over the wilted spinach then mix to scramble it.
- Once the egg is set, season with pepper then stir well.
- Transfer the scrambled egg to a serving dish then garnish with sliced tomatoes.
- Enjoy warm.

Veggie Mushroom in Cabbage Leaves

Serving: 1

Nutrition Facts
Servings: 1
Per Serving
Calories 197
Total Fat 3.6g
Saturated Fat 0.5g
Trans Fat 0g
Cholesterol 0mg
Sodium 356mg
Potassium 1087mg
Total Carb 37.9g
Dietary Fiber 9.3g
Sugars 19.1g
Protein 8.7g
Nutrition Facts
Servings: 1
Per Serving
Calories 197

Ingredients:

- 1 cup chopped mushroom
- 1 teaspoon minced garlic
- ½ teaspoon black pepper
- 1-teaspoon soy sauce
- ½ teaspoon olive oil
- ½ cup chopped red tomatoes
- 1 medium cucumber
- ½ lb. cabbage leaves

Directions:

- Preheat a skillet over medium heat then pours olive oil into it.
- Once it is hot, stir in minced garlic then sautés until wilted and aromatic.
- Next, add chopped mushroom into the skillet then season with black pepper and soy sauce. Stir well until the mushroom is wilted and completely cooked. Remove from heat then set aside.
- After that, take half of the cabbage then place in a steamer. Steam the cabbage until just soft and wilted then let it cool.
- Meanwhile, cut the cucumber into slices and chop the remaining cabbage roughly.
- Arrange the steamed cabbage on a flat surface until becoming a large layer.
- Put chopped cabbage, sliced cucumber, and chopped tomatoes on the cabbage then top with sautéed mushroom.
- Tightly roll the cabbage then place on a serving dish.
- Serve and enjoy immediately.

Lemon Grass Fish Fritter

Serving: 4

Nutrition Facts
Servings: 4
Per Serving
Calories 167
Total Fat 9.9g
Saturated Fat 3.3g
Trans Fat 0g
Cholesterol 19mg
Sodium 303mg
Potassium 252mg
Total Carb 12.4g
Dietary Fiber 0.8g
Sugars 0.3g
Protein 8.7g
Nutrition Facts
Servings: 4
Per Serving
Calories 167

Ingredients:

½ lb. fish fillet

¼ cup coconut flakes

1 teaspoon minced garlic

¼ teaspoon pepper

¼ teaspoon turmeric

¼ teaspoon ginger

4 lemon grasses

1-teaspoon olive oil

Directions:

- Preheat an oven to 425 F then coats a baking sheet with cooking oil. Set aside.
- Place all of the ingredients in a food processor then process until combined.
- Shape the mixture using your hands into medium balls then prick with lemon grasses.
- Arrange the fish satay on the prepared baking sheet then bake for about 15 minutes until lightly golden.
- Once it is done, remove from the oven and transfer to a serving dish.
- Serve and enjoy warm.

Day 3

Breakfast : Quinoa Salad Bowl
Lunch   : Macaroni Tuna Salads
Dinner   : Scrumptious Tuna Tomato

Quinoa Salad Bowl

Serving: 3

Nutrition Facts
Servings: 4
Per Serving
Calories 247
Total Fat 7.2g
Saturated Fat 3.2g
Trans Fat 0g
Cholesterol 20mg
Sodium 236mg
Potassium 359mg
Total Carb 31.7g
Dietary Fiber 3.3g
Sugars 3.5g
Protein 14.5g
Nutrition Facts
Servings: 4
Per Serving
Calories 247

Ingredients:

½ cup Greek yogurt

¼ cup chopped onion

1 teaspoon minced garlic

¼ teaspoon pepper

½ teaspoon olive oil

½ cup chopped spinach

¼ cup halved cherry tomato

½ cup feta crumbles

1 cup cooked quinoa

Directions:

- Combine yogurt with chopped onion, minced garlic, and pepper. Stir until mixed.
- Preheat a skillet over medium heat then pour olive oil into it.
- Once it is hot, stir in chopped spinach into the skillet and sautés until wilted.
- Add halved cherry tomatoes into the skillet and stir until combined with the spinach.
- Add feta crumbles and cooked quinoa into the skillet then pour the yogurt mixture over the quinoa.
- Using a wooden spatula mix until combined and completely cooked.
- Transfer the cooked quinoa to a serving dish then enjoy hot.

30 Day Mediterranean Diet Challenge

Macaroni Tuna Salads

Serving: 2

Nutrition Facts
Servings: 4
Per Serving
Calories 160
Total Fat 4.4g
Saturated Fat 0.6g
Trans Fat 0g
Cholesterol 31mg
Sodium 220mg
Potassium 135mg
Total Carb 20g
Dietary Fiber 0.3g
Sugars 0.7g
Protein 7.2g
Nutrition Facts
Servings: 4
Per Serving
Calories 160

Ingredients:

½ cup macaroni

2 tablespoons tuna chunks

2 tablespoons minced garlic

1-cup cherry tomato

¼ cup white wine

1-tablespoon olive oil

1 teaspoon lemon juice

¼ teaspoon pepper

Directions:

- Cook the macaroni according to the package direction. Drain then sets aside.
- Meanwhile, preheat a skillet over medium heat then pour olive oil into it.
- When the oil is hot, stir in minced garlic then sautés until wilted and aromatic.
- Add wine and cherry tomato then cook until the tomatoes are completely broken down.
- Next, stir in tuna chunks and drizzle lemon juice on top.
- Season with pepper then cook for about 2 minutes.
- Add the cooked pasta into the skillet then gently stir it until well mixed.
- Transfer the pasta to a serving dish then serve warm.

30 Day Mediterranean Diet Challenge

Scrumptious Tuna Tomato

Serving: 6

Nutrition Facts
Servings: 6
Per Serving
Calories 169
Total Fat 7.5g
Saturated Fat 1.4g
Trans Fat 0g
Cholesterol 23mg
Sodium 45mg
Potassium 459mg
Total Carb 3.9g
Dietary Fiber 1.1g
Sugars 2.2g
Protein 20.9g
Nutrition Facts
Servings: 6
Per Serving
Calories 169

Ingredients:

- ½ tablespoon olive oil
- 2 teaspoon minced garlic
- 2 teaspoon sliced shallots
- 4 medium red tomatoes
- ½ teaspoon ginger
- ½ teaspoon pepper
- 1 lb. tuna
- 2 cups water

Directions:

- Chop the tomatoes then place in a food processor. Process until smooth then set aside.
- Preheat a skillet over medium heat then pour olive oil into it.
- Once it is hot, stir in minced garlic and sliced shallot then sauté until lightly brown and aromatic.
- Add tuna into the skillet then season with ginger and pepper. Using a wooden spatula, carefully stir the tuna until completely seasoned.
- Pour water over the tuna then bring to boil.
- Once it is boiled, reduce the heat and continue to cook for about 15 minutes.
- After that, pour the tomato paste then bring to a simmer while stirring occasionally.
- Once it is done, remove from heat and transfer the tuna tomato to a serving bowl.
- Serve and enjoy warm.

Day 4

Breakfast : Nutritious Tuna Sandwich
Lunch : Cabbage Rolls in Brown Gravy
Dinner : Cheesy Tomato Balls

Nutritious Tuna Sandwich

Serving: 2

Nutrition Facts
Servings: 2
Per Serving
Calories 207
Total Fat 5.4g
Saturated Fat 0.9g
Trans Fat 0g
Cholesterol 15mg
Sodium 174mg
Potassium 195mg
Total Carb 20.1g
Dietary Fiber 6.4g
Sugars 3.8g
Protein 17.1g
Nutrition Facts
Servings: 2
Per Serving
Calories 207

Ingredients:

½ tablespoon olive oil

4 slices whole-grain bread

1 cup cooked tuna

2 lettuces leaves

2 slices red tomatoes

2 tablespoons chopped onion

1 ½ tablespoon low-fat mayonnaise

¼ teaspoon black pepper

Directions:

- Combine tuna with mayonnaise, chopped onion, and pepper. Mix well.
- Divide the tuna into two then shape each tuna mixture into patty form.
- Place two slices whole-grain bread on a flat surface then brush with olive oil.
- Place the tuna patties on them then layer sliced tomato and lettuce on each slice of bread.
- Top with the remaining bread then serve.
- Enjoy!

30 Day Mediterranean Diet Challenge

Cabbage Rolls in Brown Gravy

Serving: 1

Nutrition Facts
Servings: 1
Per Serving
Calories 80
Total Fat 1.8g
Saturated Fat 0.3g
Trans Fat 0g
Cholesterol 0mg
Sodium 1829mg
Potassium 288mg
Total Carb 13.9g
Dietary Fiber 3.1g
Sugars 4.9g
Protein 3.8g
Nutrition Facts
Servings: 1
Per Serving
Calories 80

Ingredients:

1-cup cabbage

½ handful leek

¼ teaspoon olive oil

1 tablespoon chopped onion

½ cup water

2 tablespoons soy sauce

¼ teaspoon sesame seeds

Directions:

- Place the cabbage in a steamer then steam over medium heat for about 5 minutes or until the cabbage is completely softened.
- Remove the cabbage from the steamer and let it cool for about 10 minutes.
- Tightly roll the cabbage then using a leek, bundle the cabbage rolls. Place the cabbage rolls in a bowl then set aside.
- Next, preheat an saucepan over medium heat then pour olive oil into it.
- Once it is hot, stir in minced garlic and sautés until wilted.
- Pour water into the saucepan and bring to boil.
- Once it is boiled, add soy sauce into the pan then bring to a simmer.
- Pour the soy gravy over the cabbage rolls then sprinkle sesame seeds on top.
- Serve and enjoy.

30 Day Mediterranean Diet Challenge

Cheesy Tomato Bowls

Serving: 4

Nutrition Facts
Servings: 4
Per Serving
Calories 198
Total Fat 7.1g
Saturated Fat 1.7g
Trans Fat 0g
Cholesterol 4mg
Sodium 417mg
Potassium 596mg
Total Carb 26.1g
Dietary Fiber 3.8g
Sugars 6.3g
Protein 8g
Nutrition Facts
Servings: 4
Per Serving
Calories 198

Ingredients:

- 4 large red tomatoes
- ½ cup couscous
- ¼ cup cauliflower florets
- 2 cups vegetable broth
- 1-tablespoon olive oil
- 1 teaspoon minced garlic
- 2 tablespoons grated cheese
- 1 tablespoon chopped celeries

Directions:

- Preheat an oven to 350 F then lines a baking sheet with parchment paper.
- Cut the top of the red tomatoes then gently remove the inside of the tomatoes.
- Place the tomatoes on the prepared baking sheet then set aside.
- Prepare a container with a lid then place couscous in it.
- Pour the vegetable broth into a pot then place on a stove over medium heat.
- Once the vegetable broth is warm, pour over the couscous. Stir well then cover with its lid. Set aside.
- Meanwhile, preheat a skillet then pour olive oil into it.
- When it is hot, stir in minced garlic then sautés until aromatic and lightly brown.
- Add cauliflower florets into the skillet then stir gently until completely wilted.
- Transfer the wilted cauliflower florets into the couscous and mix until combined.
- Fill the tomatoes with couscous mixture then sprinkles grated cheese and chopped celeries on top.
- Bake for about 15 minutes until the cheese is melted.
- When the cheesy stuffed tomatoes are done, remove them from the oven and arrange on a serving platter.
- Serve and enjoy!

Day 5

Breakfast : Easy Paprika Omelet
Lunch : Veggie Roll with Avocado
Dinner : Hot Shrimps Black Pepper

Easy Paprika Omelet

Serving: 2

Nutrition Facts
Servings: 2
Per Serving
Calories 134
Total Fat 9.5g
Saturated Fat 2.1g
Trans Fat 0g
Cholesterol 164mg
Sodium 67mg
Potassium 372mg
Total Carb 8.5g
Dietary Fiber 5g
Sugars 2.1g
Protein 7.5g
Nutrition Facts
Servings: 2
Per Serving
Calories 134

Ingredients:

2 organic eggs

2 tablespoons water

¼ teaspoon pepper

1 ½ teaspoons olive oil

¼ cup chopped red paprika

2 tablespoons chopped onion

Directions:

- Crack the eggs and place in a medium bowl.
- Pour water into the eggs then season with pepper. Mix well.
- Add chopped red paprika and onion into the egg mixture the stir until combined.
- Preheat a non-stick skillet over medium heat then brush with olive oil.
- Once it is hot, pour the egg mixture then cooks for a few minutes until sets.
- Flip the egg and cook again until both sides are completely cooked and lightly brown.
- Remove from the skillet then transfer to a platter.
- Serve and enjoy.

Veggie Roll with Avocado

Serving: 2

Nutrition Facts
Servings: 2
Per Serving
Calories 286
Total Fat 16.2g
Saturated Fat 1.9g
Trans Fat 0g
Cholesterol 0mg
Sodium 283mg
Potassium 170mg
Total Carb 33.8g
Dietary Fiber 9.3g
Sugars 8.7g
Protein 4.6g
Nutrition Facts
Servings: 2
Per Serving
Calories 286

Ingredients:

- 1-cup fresh lettuce
- ½ cup shredded carrots
- ½ cup cucumber sticks
- ¼ cup chopped radish
- 1 cup avocado wedges
- 1 tablespoon lemon juice
- 2 whole-grain tortillas

Directions:

- Arrange fresh lettuce on a place next to carrot, cucumber, and radish.
- Drizzle lemon juice over the vegetables and let them sit for about a minute until the lemon juice is completely absorbed.
- Place the tortillas on a flat surface then arrange avocado wedges on each tortilla.
- Layer with lettuce, carrots, cucumber, and radish then tightly wrap the tortillas.
- Transfer the tortillas to a container then have your lunch.

Hot Shrimps Black Pepper

Serving: 2

Nutrition Facts
Servings: 2
Per Serving
Calories 172
Total Fat 3.5g
Saturated Fat 0.9g
Trans Fat 0g
Cholesterol 269mg
Sodium 314mg
Potassium 273mg
Total Carb 4.4g
Dietary Fiber 0.9g
Sugars 1.2g
Protein 29.4g
Nutrition Facts
Servings: 2
Per Serving
Calories 172

Ingredients:

- 1-cup fresh shrimps
- 2 tablespoons chopped red chili
- ½ teaspoon olive oil
- ½ teaspoon black pepper
- 1 tablespoon chopped onion

Directions:

- Remove the shrimps 'head then set aside.
- Preheat a skillet over medium heat then pours olive oil into it.

- Once it is hot, stir in chopped onion then sautés until lightly brown and aromatic.
- Add red chili flakes then sautés until just wilted.
- Next, toss fresh shrimps into the skillet then season with black pepper. Stir well until the shrimps are pink and completely cooked.
- Transfer the sautéed shrimps to a serving dish. Enjoy!

Day 6

Breakfast : Almond Overnight Oats
Lunch : Beautiful Mixed Salads
Dinner : Potato Lentils Stew

Almond Overnight Oats

Serving: 4

Nutrition Facts
Servings: 4
Per Serving
Calories 166
Total Fat 15.4g
Saturated Fat 12.8g
Trans Fat 0g
Cholesterol 0mg
Sodium 9mg
Potassium 187mg
Total Carb 7.1g
Dietary Fiber 2g
Sugars 2.1g
Protein 2.4g
Nutrition Facts
Servings: 4
Per Serving
Calories 166

Ingredients:

¼ cup rolled oats

1 cup almond milk

1 tablespoon chopped roasted almonds

Additional fruits, as desired

Directions:

- Place the oats in a jar then pour the milk into the jar.
- Seal the jar with its lid then stores in the refrigerator over night.
- In the morning, remove the oats from the refrigerator then open the lid.
- Transfer the soaked oats to a saucepan over medium heat and cook until warm.
- Pour the oats to a serving bowl then add any kind of fruits as you desired and sprinkle chopped roasted almond on top.
- Serve and enjoy immediately.

30 Day Mediterranean Diet Challenge

Beautiful Mixed Salads

Serving: 2

Nutrition Facts
Servings: 2
Per Serving
Calories 144
Total Fat 0.8g
Saturated Fat 0.2g
Trans Fat 0g
Cholesterol 0mg
Sodium 4mg
Potassium 431mg
Total Carb 35.9g
Dietary Fiber 4.4g
Sugars 30.2g
Protein 2g
Nutrition Facts
Servings: 2
Per Serving
Calories 144

Ingredients:

½ cup cubed cucumber

½ cup cubed apple

½ cup shredded carrot

1 cup chopped lettuce

¼ cup chopped tomato

1 tablespoon lemon juice

1-teaspoon vinegar

Directions:

- Place all of the vegetables and fruits in a salad bowl then splash lemon juice and vinegar on top.
- Carefully mix all ingredients until all of them are completely seasoned with lemon juice and vinegar.
- Enjoy immediately or chill in the refrigerator if you want to consume it later.

Potato Lentils Stew

Serving: 3

Nutrition Facts
Servings: 3
Per Serving
Calories 169
Total Fat 1.8g
Saturated Fat 0.6g
Trans Fat 0g
Cholesterol 0mg
Sodium 431mg
Potassium 544mg
Total Carb 26.8g
Dietary Fiber 11.2g
Sugars 2.9g
Protein 11.6g
Nutrition Facts
Servings: 3
Per Serving
Calories 169

Ingredients:

½ cup lentils

1 ½ cups vegetable broth

½ cup cubed potatoes

½ cup diced tomatoes

¼ cup diced carrot

3 tablespoons chopped onion

½ tablespoon chopped parsley

1 teaspoon minced garlic

½ teaspoon pepper

Directions:

- Wash and rinse the lentils.
- Discard the water then place the lentils in a saucepan.
- Add tomatoes, potatoes, and carrot into the saucepan then pour vegetable broth into the saucepan.
- Stir in onion and parsley then season with garlic and pepper.
- Bring to a simmer for about 45 minutes or until the lentils are soft. Stir well.
- Transfer to a serving dish then serve warm.

Day 7

Breakfast : Original Banana Pancake
Lunch   : Zucchini Spaghetti Black Pepper
Dinner   : Veggie Mixed Quinoa

Original Banana Pancake

Serving: 4

Nutrition Facts
Servings: 4
Per Serving
Calories 195
Total Fat 11.3g
Saturated Fat 9.6g
Trans Fat 0g
Cholesterol 0mg
Sodium 7mg
Potassium 160mg
Total Carb 21.5g
Dietary Fiber 1.7g
Sugars 2.1g
Protein 3.5g
Nutrition Facts
Servings: 4
Per Serving
Calories 195

Ingredients:

¾ cup whole-wheat flour

¾ cup almond milk

2 tablespoons mashed banana

¼ teaspoon olive oil

Directions:

- Place the whole-wheat flour in a bowl then make a hole in the center of the bowl.
- Pour almond milk into the hole then using a whisker, combine the ingredients until smooth.
- Next, add mashed banana into the mixture and continue whisking until well mixed.
- Preheat a frying pan over medium heat the brush olive oil over the surface.
- Once it is hot, pour the batter on the hot pan.
- Cook for about a minute then flip the pancake.
- Continue to cook the pancake until the pancake is completely cooked and both sides are lightly brown.
- Place the pancake on a serving platter then enjoy.

Zucchini Spaghetti Black Pepper

Serving: 2

Nutrition Facts
Servings: 2
Per Serving
Calories 127
Total Fat 7.5g
Saturated Fat 1.1g
Trans Fat 0g
Cholesterol 10mg
Sodium 301mg
Potassium 246mg
Total Carb 13.5g
Dietary Fiber 1.1g
Sugars 1.8g
Protein 2.9g
Nutrition Facts
Servings: 2
Per Serving
Calories 127

Ingredients:

- 1 oz. uncooked spaghetti
- ½ cup sliced zucchini
- 2 tablespoons minced garlic
- ½ cup cherry tomatoes
- 1-tablespoon olive oil
- ¼ teaspoon black pepper

Directions:

- Cook the spaghetti according to the package direction. Drain then sets aside.

- Meanwhile, preheat a skillet over medium heat then pour olive oil into it.
- When the oil is hot, stir in minced garlic then sautés until wilted and aromatic.
- Add cherry tomatoes and sliced zucchini then cook until the vegetables are wilted.
- Season with black pepper then cook for about 2 minutes.
- Add the cooked spaghetti into the skillet then gently stir it until well mixed.
- Transfer the pasta to a serving dish then serve warm.

Veggie Mixed Quinoa

Serving: 4

Nutrition Facts
Servings: 4
Per Serving
Calories 244
Total Fat 9.6g
Saturated Fat 1.3g
Trans Fat 0g
Cholesterol 2mg
Sodium 29mg
Potassium 376mg
Total Carb 31.2g
Dietary Fiber 3.8g
Sugars 2.3g
Protein 9.3g
Nutrition Facts
Servings: 4
Per Serving
Calories 244

Ingredients:

- 1 cup cooked quinoa
- ½ cup Greek yogurt
- 2 tablespoons olive oil
- ¼ cup chopped onion
- 1 teaspoon minced garlic
- 1 cup chopped spinach
- ½ cup chopped carrot
- ¼ cup chopped cabbage

Directions:

- Preheat a skillet over medium heat then pour olive oil into it.
- Once it is hot, stir in chopped onion and minced garlic then sautés until wilted and aromatic.
- Add the spinach, carrot, and cabbage into the skillet then sauté until cooked.
- Next, pour yogurt into the skillet and stir well.
- After that, stir in the cooked quinoa into the skillet and stir vigorously until the mixture is completely combined.
- Once is done, transfer to a serving dish then serves immediately.

Day 8

Breakfast : Potato Hash Black Pepper
Lunch : Summer Veggie Roll
Dinner : Spiced Chicken Satay

Potato Hash Black Pepper

Serving: 2

Nutrition Facts
Servings: 2
Per Serving
Calories 212
Total Fat 14.2g
Saturated Fat 2.1g
Trans Fat 0g
Cholesterol 0mg
Sodium 42mg
Potassium 383mg
Total Carb 21g
Dietary Fiber 2.9g
Sugars 1.3g
Protein 2.7g
Nutrition Facts
Servings: 2
Per Serving
Calories 212

Ingredients:

2 cups cubes potatoes

½ cup cubed pumpkin

4 tablespoons chopped onion

1 ½ teaspoons ginger

½ teaspoon black pepper

2 tablespoons olive oil

Directions:

- Preheat a skillet over medium heat then pour olive oil into it.
- Once it is hot, stir in chopped onion then sautés until wilted and aromatic.
- Next, add cubed potatoes into the skillet then season with ginger.
- Reduce the heat and cook the potatoes for about 5 minutes until the potatoes are completely cooked but still crispy.
- After that, stir in cubed pumpkin and sprinkle black pepper over the mixture. Stir well.
- Transfer the potato hash to a serving platter then enjoy warm.

Summer Veggie Roll

Serving: 4

Nutrition Facts
Servings: 4
Per Serving
Calories 168
Total Fat 2.1g
Saturated Fat 0.3g
Trans Fat 0g
Cholesterol 0mg
Sodium 11mg
Potassium 28mg
Total Carb 29.9g
Dietary Fiber 4.9g
Sugars 8.5g
Protein 4.6g
Nutrition Facts
Servings: 4
Per Serving
Calories 168

Ingredients:

½ cup whole-grain flour

1-½ cup water

½ teaspoon black pepper

1-cup fresh lettuce

1 cup chopped red tomatoes

1 tablespoon lemon juice

½ teaspoon olive oil

Directions:

- Place whole-grain flour in a bowl then pours water into it.
- Season with black pepper then using a whisker, combine the flour with water until incorporated.
- Preheat a pan over medium heat then brush with olive oil.
- Once it is hot, pour a scoop of the flour mixture then shake until the mixture spread evenly—shape like tortilla but soft.
- Cook for a few minutes then transfer the soft tortilla on a plate.
- Repeat with the remaining batter then place the tortillas on a flat surface.
- Meanwhile, place the chopped red tomatoes and chopped lettuce in a bowl then drizzle lemon juice over the veggie. Using two forks, mix the veggie until combined.
- Next, divide the veggie mixture into four then drop on each tortilla.
- After that, roll the tortillas tightly then serve on a serving platter.
- Enjoy!

Spiced Chicken Satay

Serving: 1

Nutrition Facts
Servings: 1
Per Serving
Calories 312
Total Fat 22.3g
Saturated Fat 3.1g
Trans Fat 0g
Cholesterol 55mg
Sodium 1486mg
Potassium 142mg
Total Carb 6.4g
Dietary Fiber 1.1g
Sugars 1.3g
Protein 24.9g
Nutrition Facts
Servings: 1
Per Serving
Calories 312

Ingredients:

3 teaspoons olive oil

1 teaspoon minced garlic

½ teaspoon coriander

½ teaspoon ginger

¼ teaspoon pepper

1-tablespoon soy sauce

1-cup cubed chicken breast

1 tablespoon chopped red chili

1 tablespoon sliced shallot

Directions:

- Combine minced garlic, coriander, ginger, and pepper in a bowl then mix until incorporated.
- Add the cubed chicken into the bowl then rub with the spices mixture. Let it sit for about 10 minutes.
- Preheat an oven to 400 F then coats a baking sheet with cooking spray. Set aside.
- Place soy sauce and olive oil in a flat platter then mix until incorporated.
- Prick the spiced chicken cubes with wooden skewers then brush them with soy sauce mixture.
- Arrange the chicken satay on the prepared baking sheet then bake for about 15 minutes until tender.
- Removes from the oven then transfer to a serving platter.
- Sprinkle sliced shallots and red chilies over the satay then enjoy warm.

30 Day Mediterranean Diet Challenge

Day 9

Breakfast : Olive Veggie Frittata
Lunch : 3 Minutes Broccoli Garlic
Dinner : The Pumpkin Pot

Olive Veggie Frittata

Serving: 2

Nutrition Facts
Servings: 2
Per Serving
Calories 100
Total Fat 6.9g
Saturated Fat 2.4g
Trans Fat 0g
Cholesterol 169mg
Sodium 227mg
Potassium 166mg
Total Carb 2.7g
Dietary Fiber 1g
Sugars 1.2g
Protein 8g
Nutrition Facts
Servings: 2
Per Serving
Calories 100

Ingredients:

2 organic eggs

4 tablespoons Greek yogurt

4 tablespoons diced tomatoes

2 tablespoons olive

½ cup chopped spinach

2 tablespoons feta crumbles

¼ teaspoon pepper

Directions:

- Preheat an oven to 350 F then coats a small casserole dish with cooking spray.
- Crack the eggs then place in a bowl. Using a whisker, whisk the eggs until fluffy.
- Add the remaining ingredients into the bowl then stir until combined.
- Pour the egg mixture into the coated casserole dish then spread evenly.
- Bake for about 15 minutes until the egg is set.
- Once it is done, remove from the oven and let it cool for a few minutes
- Serve and enjoy warm.

3 Minutes Broccoli Garlic

Serving: 2

Nutrition Facts
Servings: 1
Per Serving
Calories 66
Total Fat 2.7g
Saturated Fat 0.4g
Trans Fat 0g
Cholesterol 0mg
Sodium 32mg
Potassium 335mg
Total Carb 9.5g
Dietary Fiber 2.8g
Sugars 1.6g
Protein 3.2g
Nutrition Facts
Servings: 1
Per Serving
Calories 66

Ingredients:

1-cup fresh chopped broccoli

½ teaspoon olive oil

½ teaspoon black pepper

3 teaspoons minced garlic

Directions:

- Preheat a skillet over medium heat then pours olive oil into it.
- Once it is hot, stir in minced garlic then sautés until lightly brown and aromatic.

- Next, toss chopped broccoli into the skillet then season with black pepper. Stir well until the broccoli is tender enough but still crispy.
- Transfer the sautéed broccoli to a serving dish. Enjoy!

The Pumpkin Pot

Serving: 4

Nutrition Facts
Servings: 4
Per Serving
Calories 175
Total Fat 5.5g
Saturated Fat 0.9g
Trans Fat 0g
Cholesterol 0mg
Sodium 19mg
Potassium 596mg
Total Carb 27.7g
Dietary Fiber 8.6g
Sugars 8.3g
Protein 6.7g
Nutrition Facts
Servings: 4
Per Serving
Calories 175

Ingredients:

¼ cup chopped onion

¼ teaspoon pepper

2 cups water

2 cups chopped pumpkin

1 cup chopped tomato

½ cup cooked chickpeas

1-tablespoon olive oil

1 tablespoon lemon juice

Directions:

- Preheat a pan over medium heat then pour olive oil into the pot.
- Once it is hot, stir in chopped onion and sautés until wilted and aromatic.
- Pour water into the pan then bring to boil.
- When it is boiled, add chopped pumpkin together with chopped tomatoes and chickpeas.
- Splash lemon juice over the vegetables then brings to a simmer for approximately 20 minutes.
- Transfer the pumpkin stew into an empty pumpkin then serve hot.

Day 10

Breakfast : Minty Avocado Greenies
Lunch : Tomato Green Peas Pizza
Dinner : Quick Chickpeas Curry

Minty Avocado Greenies

Serving: 3

Nutrition Facts
Servings: 3
Per Serving
Calories 261
Total Fat 20.5g
Saturated Fat 4.4g
Trans Fat 0.2g
Cholesterol 0mg
Sodium 134mg
Potassium 84mg
Total Carb 13.7g
Dietary Fiber 5.5g
Sugars 2.2g
Protein 5.6g
Nutrition Facts
Servings: 3
Per Serving
Calories 261

Ingredients:

2 ripe avocados

3 teaspoons chopped mint leaves

1 tablespoon lemon juice

3 slices whole-wheat bread

Directions:

- Cut the avocados into halves then discard the seeds.
- Next, using a spoon, dredge the avocados then place in a bowl.
- Drizzle lemon juice over the avocados then add mint leaves into it. Mix until combined.
- Toast the whole-wheat bread until golden.
- Once it is done, places the whole-wheat bread on a serving platter then spreads the avocado on each slice.
- Serve and enjoy warm.

Tomato Green Peas Pizza

Serving: 8

Nutrition Facts
Servings: 8
Per Serving
Calories 166
Total Fat 13.4g
Saturated Fat 3g
Trans Fat 0g
Cholesterol 8mg
Sodium 241mg
Potassium 46mg
Total Carb 6.9g
Dietary Fiber 1.6g
Sugars 3.1g
Protein 4.9g
Nutrition Facts
Servings: 8
Per Serving
Calories 166

Ingredients:

1 whole-wheat pizza crust

1-cup pesto sauce

1-cup halved cherry tomato

½ cup green peas

½ cup grated Mozzarella cheese

Directions:

- Preheat an oven to 350 F then coat a pizza pan with cooking spray.

- Drizzle pesto sauce on the pizza crust then spread evenly.
- Place cherry tomatoes and green peas on the top then cover with grated Mozzarella cheese.
- Bake for approximately 10 minutes or until the cheese is melted.
- Remove from the oven then serve warm.

Quick Chickpeas Curry

Serving: 4

Nutrition Facts
Servings: 4
Per Serving
Calories 206
Total Fat 3.7g
Saturated Fat 0.4g
Trans Fat 0g
Cholesterol 0mg
Sodium 126mg
Potassium 467mg
Total Carb 34.2g
Dietary Fiber 9.6g
Sugars 7.1g
Protein 10.4g
Nutrition Facts
Servings: 4
Per Serving
Calories 206

Ingredients:

1 cup cooked chickpeas

2 tablespoons chopped onion

1 teaspoon minced garlic

½ teaspoon ginger

1-teaspoon curry powder

1 cup diced red tomatoes

½ teaspoon turmeric

2 cups water

½ teaspoon olive oil

Directions:

- Preheat a pan over medium heat then pour olive oil into it.
- Once it is hot, stir in chopped onion and minced garlic into the pan then sauté until wilted and aromatic.
- Next, add the cooked chickpeas then season with ginger, curry powder, and turmeric. Stir well.
- Toss in the diced tomatoes and cook until the tomatoes are tender.
- After that, pour water into the pan and bring to boil.
- Once it is boiled, reduce the heat and cook until the water is completely absorbed into the chickpeas.
- Remove from heat then transfer the chickpeas curry to a serving bowl.
- Garnish with any green, as you desired.

30 Day Mediterranean Diet Challenge

Day 11

Breakfast : Banana and Dates Oat Porridge
Lunch   : Avocado Chickpeas Curry Salads
Dinner   : Delicious Chicken in Tomato Sauce

Banana and Dates Oat Porridge

Serving: 2

Nutrition Facts
Servings: 2
Per Serving
Calories 162
Total Fat 1.6g
Saturated Fat 0.3g
Trans Fat 0g
Cholesterol 0mg
Sodium 9mg
Potassium 362mg
Total Carb 35.9g
Dietary Fiber 4.6g
Sugars 14.5g
Protein 3.6g
Nutrition Facts
Servings: 2
Per Serving
Calories 162

Ingredients:

2 cups water

½ cup oatmeal

1 medium banana

2 tablespoons chopped dates

¼ teaspoon cinnamon

Directions:

- Peel and cut the banana into slices then set aside.
- Pour water in a saucepan then bring to boil.
- Once it is boiled, stir in oatmeal over the boiling water. Stir until combined.
- Reduce the heat then bring to a simmer for about 15 minutes.
- After that, add sliced banana and dates into the saucepan then stir for a few seconds.
- Transfer the oats porridge to a serving bowl and sprinkle cinnamon on top.
- Serve and enjoy warm

Avocado Chickpeas Curry Salads

Serving: 8

Nutrition Facts
Servings: 8
Per Serving
Calories 237
Total Fat 12.2g
Saturated Fat 2.7g
Trans Fat 0g
Cholesterol 1mg
Sodium 75mg
Potassium 562mg
Total Carb 25.4g
Dietary Fiber 8.9g
Sugars 6.9g
Protein 9g
Nutrition Facts
Servings: 8
Per Serving
Calories 237

Ingredients:

- 2 ripe avocados
- 1 cup chopped orange
- 1 cup green collard or any green, as you desired
- ½ teaspoon pepper
- 2 tablespoons Greek yogurt
- 1 cup cooked chickpeas
- 2 tablespoons chopped onion
- 1 teaspoon minced garlic
- ½ teaspoon ginger
- 1-teaspoon curry powder

1 cup diced red tomatoes

½ teaspoon turmeric

2 cups water

½ teaspoon olive oil

Directions:

- First, cook the chickpeas curry.
- Preheat a pan over medium heat then pour olive oil into it.
- Once it is hot, stir in chopped onion and minced garlic into the pan then sauté until wilted and aromatic.
- Next, add the cooked chickpeas then season with ginger, curry powder, and turmeric. Stir well.
- Toss in the diced tomatoes and cook until the tomatoes are tender.
- After that, pour water into the pan and bring to boil.
- Once it is boiled, reduce the heat and cook until the water is completely absorbed into the chickpeas.
- Remove from heat then transfer the chickpeas curry to a serving bowl. Let it cool.
- Meanwhile, peel and cut the avocados and orange into cubes then toss into the chickpeas bowl.
- Sprinkle pepper over the salads then using two forks mix until combined.

- Drop Greek yogurt on the top then serves immediately.

30 Day Mediterranean Diet Challenge

Delicious Chicken in Tomato Sauce

Serving: 2

Nutrition Facts
Servings: 2
Per Serving
Calories 150
Total Fat 7.8g
Saturated Fat 1.5g
Trans Fat 0g
Cholesterol 38mg
Sodium 44mg
Potassium 385mg
Total Carb 6.4g
Dietary Fiber 1.7g
Sugars 2.9g
Protein 14g
Nutrition Facts
Servings: 2
Per Serving
Calories 150

Ingredients:

½ tablespoon olive oil

2 teaspoon minced garlic

2 tablespoons chopped onion

½ teaspoon pepper

1 lb. organic chicken breast

1 cup diced tomatoes

1-teaspoon sesame seeds

1 tablespoon chopped leek

Directions:

- Cut the chicken breast into medium cubes then set aside.
- Preheat olive oil in a skillet over medium heat.
- Once it is hot, stir in minced garlic and chopped onion then sauté until aromatic and lightly brown.
- Next, add the cubed chicken into the skillet then season with pepper.
- Toss in the diced tomatoes and stir occasionally until the chicken is completely cooked.
- Transfer the cooked chicken to a serving dish then sprinkle chopped leek and sesame seeds on top.
- Serve and enjoy warm.

Day 12

Breakfast : Coconut Blueberry Stones
Lunch : Fruity Beans Salads
Dinner : Beef Meat Balls in Red Gravy

Coconut Blueberry Scones

Serving: 4

Nutrition Facts
Servings: 4
Per Serving
Calories 129
Total Fat 8.7g
Saturated Fat 4g
Trans Fat 0g
Cholesterol 1mg
Sodium 17mg
Potassium 146mg
Total Carb 10.3g
Dietary Fiber 3.3g
Sugars 5.4g
Protein 4.5g
Nutrition Facts
Servings: 4
Per Serving
Calories 129

Ingredients:

1-cup coconut flour

2-½ tablespoons almond butter

1-cup fresh blueberries

5 tablespoons Greek yogurt

4 tablespoons coconut milk

Directions:

- Preheat an oven to 425 F then lines a baking sheet with parchment paper.
- Place the whole-wheat flour in a bowl then adds sliced almond butter into the bowl.
- Slowly pour Greek yogurt, and coconut milk into the bowl then knead until becoming dough.
- After that, stir in fresh blueberries then mix until combined.
- Form the dough into small patties then arrange on the prepared baking sheet.
- Bake for approximately 15 minutes or until the scones are lightly golden.
- Remove the scones from the heat then transfer to a serving dish.
- Serve and enjoy.

Fruity Beans Salads

Serving: 4

Nutrition Facts
Servings: 4
Per Serving
Calories 295
Total Fat 10.5g
Saturated Fat 2.2g
Trans Fat 0g
Cholesterol 0mg
Sodium 14mg
Potassium 975mg
Total Carb 41.8g
Dietary Fiber 12.1g
Sugars 7.5g
Protein 11.5g
Nutrition Facts
Servings: 4
Per Serving
Calories 295

Ingredients:

1 fresh apple

1 ripe avocado

½ cup cooked pinto beans

½ cup cooked red beans

¼ cup chopped celery

1 tablespoon unsweetened orange juice

Directions:

- Cut the apples into cubes the place in a bowl.

- Peel the avocado and discard the seed then cut into small cubes.
- Place the avocado cubes into the same bowl with the cubed apple then add the beans into the bowl.
- Pour unsweetened orange juice over the salads then using two forks mix the ingredients until combined.
- Let it sit for about an hour in the refrigerator until the orange juice is completely absorbed into the beans and fruits.
- Once you want to enjoy, remove from the refrigerator then sprinkle chopped celeries on top.
- Enjoy as your healthy lunch.

Beef Meat Balls in Red Gravy

Serving: 4

Nutrition Facts
Servings: 5
Per Serving
Calories 240
Total Fat 11.7g
Saturated Fat 7.3g
Trans Fat 0g
Cholesterol 81mg
Sodium 69mg
Potassium 474mg
Total Carb 4.4g
Dietary Fiber 1.2g
Sugars 1.7g
Protein 28.5g
Nutrition Facts
Servings: 5
Per Serving
Calories 240

Ingredients:

1 lb. ground beef

1-tablespoon whole-wheat flour

¼ cup red chili

1 teaspoon sliced garlic

1 teaspoon sliced shallots

2 tablespoons chopped leek

2 cups water

½ cup coconut milk

¼ teaspoon olive oil

Directions:

- Place the ground beef and the whole-wheat flour in a food processor then process until smooth.
- Shape into medium balls then set aside.
- Preheat a saucepan over medium heat then pour olive oil into it.
- Once it is hot, stir in sliced garlic and shallot then sauté until aromatic.
- Pour water into the saucepan then bring to boil.
- Once it is boiled, carefully place the meatballs in the saucepan then cook until the balls set.
- Pour coconut milk over the balls then bring to a simmer for approximately 7 minutes.
- Sprinkle chopped leek into the pan then stir until just mixed.
- Transfer the meatballs together with the gravy to a serving dish.
- Serve and enjoy warm.

Day 13

Breakfast : Fresh Blueberry Dorayaki
Lunch : Spicy Vegetable Curry in Blanket
Dinner : Scrumptious Spinach Balls

Fresh Blueberry Dorayaki

Serving: 4

Nutrition Facts
Servings: 4
Per Serving
Calories 196
Total Fat 11.3g
Saturated Fat 9.6g
Trans Fat 0g
Cholesterol 0mg
Sodium 7mg
Potassium 150mg
Total Carb 21.7g
Dietary Fiber 1.8g
Sugars 2.5g
Protein 3.5g
Nutrition Facts
Servings: 4
Per Serving
Calories 196

Ingredients:

¾ cup whole-wheat flour

¾ cup almond milk

¼ cup fresh blueberries

¼ teaspoon olive oil

Directions:

- Place the fresh blueberries in a blender then blend until smooth.
- Transfer the smooth blueberry to a container with a lid then chill in the refrigerator.
- Meanwhile, place the whole-wheat flour in a bowl then make a hole in the center of the bowl.
- Pour almond milk into the hole then using a whisker, combine the ingredients until smooth.
- Preheat a frying pan over medium heat the brush olive oil over the surface.
- Once it is hot, pour half of the batter on the hot pan.
- Cook for about a minute then flip the pancake.
- Continue to cook the pancake until the pancake is completely cooked and both sides are lightly brown.
- Place the pancake on a serving platter then repeat with the remaining batter.
- Remove the blueberry from the refrigerator then drop it on the pancake.
- Cover with the other pancake on top then enjoy immediately.

30 Day Mediterranean Diet Challenge

Spicy Vegetable Curry in Blanket

Serving: 6

Nutrition Facts
Servings: 6
Per Serving
Calories 277
Total Fat 18.9g
Saturated Fat 12.2g
Trans Fat 0.3g
Cholesterol 8mg
Sodium 582mg
Potassium 183mg
Total Carb 23g
Dietary Fiber 5g
Sugars 3.4g
Protein 4.4g
Nutrition Facts
Servings: 6
Per Serving
Calories 277

Ingredients:

½ cup whole-grain flour

1-½ cup water

½ teaspoon black pepper

1 cup chopped eggplant

½ cup shredded carrot

½ cup chopped cabbage

1 tablespoon red chili flakes

1 tablespoon green chili flakes

½ teaspoon olive oil

½ teaspoon minced garlic

½ teaspoon sliced shallot

½ teaspoon curry

1-cup coconut milk

Directions:

- Place whole-grain flour in a bowl then pours water into it.
- Season with black pepper then using a whisker, combine the flour with water until incorporated.
- Preheat a pan over medium heat then brush with olive oil.
- Once it is hot, pour a scoop of the flour mixture then shake until the mixture spread evenly—shape like tortilla but soft.
- Cook for a few minutes then transfer the soft tortilla on a plate.
- Repeat with the remaining batter then place the tortillas on a flat surface.
- Meanwhile, preheat a saucepan over medium heat then pour olive oil into it.
- Once it is hot, stir in minced garlic and shallots then sauté until wilted and aromatic.
- Add red chili, green chili, and curry then toss the chopped vegetables into the pan. Continue cooking until the vegetable is wilted and tender.
- Pour coconut milk into the pan and bring to a simmer until the coconut milk is completely absorbed into the vegetables.
- Drop the vegetable curry on the prepared whole-grain tortillas then fold them.

- The Spicy vegetable Curry in Blanket is ready to be enjoyed.

Scrumptious Spinach Balls

Serving: 1

Nutrition Facts
Servings: 1
Per Serving
Calories 195
Total Fat 1.5g
Saturated Fat 0.4g
Trans Fat 0g
Cholesterol 0mg
Sodium 47mg
Potassium 156mg
Total Carb 32.1g
Dietary Fiber 6.9g
Sugars 0.3g
Protein 10.1g
Nutrition Facts
Servings: 1
Per Serving
Calories 195

Ingredients:

- ½ cup whole-grain flour
- ½ cup chopped spinach
- 1 organic egg white
- 2 tablespoons water
- 1-½ teaspoons minced garlic
- ¼ teaspoon pepper

Directions:

- Place all ingredients in a bowl then using your hand mix well until becoming dough.

- Shape the dough into medium balls form then places them in a steamer over medium heat.
- Cook the spinach balls for about 20 minutes then take them out from the steamer.
- Transfer the spinach balls to a serving bowl then enjoy warm.

Day 14

Breakfast : Cheese Tomato Sandwich
Lunch : Mediterranean Lentils Black Pepper
Dinner : Spicy Spaghetti Veggie

Cheese Tomato Sandwich

Serving: 1

Nutrition Facts
Servings: 1
Per Serving
Calories 245
Total Fat 3.1g
Saturated Fat 1.2g
Trans Fat 0g
Cholesterol 6mg
Sodium 424mg
Potassium 154mg
Total Carb 36.1g
Dietary Fiber 11g
Sugars 8.2g
Protein 15.5g
Nutrition Facts
Servings: 1
Per Serving
Calories 245

Ingredients:

½ tablespoon olive oil

2 slices whole-grain bread

¼ cup sliced tomatoes

2 tablespoons chopped onion

1 slice cheese

Directions:

- Preheat a saucepan over medium heat then brushes the saucepan with olive oil.
- Once it is hot, place the whole-wheat bread on the saucepan. Let the bread on the saucepan and flip until both sides are lightly brown.
- Remove the bread from the pan and place a slice of bread on a platter.
- Layer cheese, onion, and tomatoes on the bread and cover with the remaining bread.
- Serve and enjoy immediately.

Mediterranean Lentils Black Pepper

Serving: 4

Nutrition Facts
Servings: 4
Per Serving
Calories 162
Total Fat 7.4g
Saturated Fat 1.1g
Trans Fat 0g
Cholesterol 0mg
Sodium 14mg
Potassium 339mg
Total Carb 18.3g
Dietary Fiber 8.3g
Sugars 2.2g
Protein 6.7g
Nutrition Facts
Servings: 4
Per Serving
Calories 162

Ingredients:

½ cup lentils

½ cup cubed carrots

½ cup chopped onion

1 teaspoon minced garlic

1-teaspoon bay leaf

½ teaspoon thyme

2 cups water

3 teaspoons lemon juice

1 tablespoon chopped parsley

½ teaspoon black pepper

2 tablespoons olive oil

¼ cup chopped tomatoes

Directions:

- Place lentils in a saucepan together with carrots, chopped onion, minced garlic, bay leaf, and thyme then pour water to cover the lentils.
- Bring to boil over medium heat and once it is boiled, reduce the heat and bring to a simmer without its cover until the lentils are tender—usually it's about 15 minutes.
- Discard the water then pour olive oil over the lentils.
- Splash lemon juice and season with parsley and black pepper.
- At last, stir in chopped tomatoes into the saucepan and stir until just mixed.
- Transfer the lentils to a serving dish then enjoy!

30 Day Mediterranean Diet Challenge

Spicy Spaghetti Veggie

Serving: 2

Nutrition Facts
Servings: 2
Per Serving
Calories 154
Total Fat 2.9g
Saturated Fat 0.3g
Trans Fat 0g
Cholesterol 10mg
Sodium 165mg
Potassium 313mg
Total Carb 26.4g
Dietary Fiber 5.7g
Sugars 5g
Protein 6.6g
Nutrition Facts
Servings: 2
Per Serving
Calories 154

Ingredients:

1 oz. uncooked spaghetti

¼ cup sliced mushroom

2 tablespoons corn kernels

2 tablespoons cooked lentils

3 tablespoons red chili flakes

2 tablespoons chopped parsley

2 tablespoons chopped onion

½ cup cherry tomatoes

1-tablespoon olive oil

¼ teaspoon pepper

Directions:

- Cook the spaghetti according to the package direction. Drain then sets aside.
- Meanwhile, preheat a skillet over medium heat then pour olive oil into it.
- When the oil is hot, stir in chopped onion and chili flakes then sauté until wilted and aromatic.
- Add cherry tomatoes, mushroom, corn kernels, and lentils then cook until the wilted and combined.
- Season with pepper then cook for about 2 minutes.
- Add the cooked spaghetti into the skillet then gently stir it until well mixed.
- Transfer the pasta to a serving dish then garnish with chopped parsley.
- Enjoy immediately.

Day 15

Breakfast : Pineapple and Tomato Quinoa
Lunch : Baked Potato Patties
Dinner : Warm Zucchini Soup

Pineapple and Tomato Quinoa

Serving: 3

Nutrition Facts
Servings: 3
Per Serving
Calories 258
Total Fat 4.6g
Saturated Fat 0.8g
Trans Fat 0g
Cholesterol 2mg
Sodium 25mg
Potassium 491mg
Total Carb 44.5g
Dietary Fiber 4.9g
Sugars 5.9g
Protein 10g
Nutrition Facts
Servings: 3
Per Serving
Calories 258

Ingredients:

½ cup low fat milk

¼ cup chopped onion

1 teaspoon minced garlic

½ teaspoon olive oil

½ cup pineapple chunks

¼ cup halved cherry tomato

1 cup cooked quinoa

Directions:

- Combine low-fat milk with chopped onion, minced garlic, and pepper. Stir until mixed.
- Preheat a skillet over medium heat then pour olive oil into it.
- Once it is hot, stir in chopped spinach into the skillet and sautés until wilted.
- Pour the milk mixture into the skillet then bring to boil.
- Once it is boiled, add feta crumbles and the cooked quinoa.
- Using a wooden spatula mix until combined and completely cooked.
- Stir in halved cherry tomatoes and pineapple chunks into the quinoa and mix well.
- Transfer the cooked quinoa to a serving dish then enjoy hot.

Baked Potato Patties

Serving: 2

Nutrition Facts
Servings: 2
Per Serving
Calories 102
Total Fat 2.5g
Saturated Fat 0.4g
Trans Fat 0g
Cholesterol 0mg
Sodium 7mg
Potassium 477mg
Total Carb 18.6g
Dietary Fiber 2.9g
Sugars 1.3g
Protein 2.1g
Nutrition Facts
Servings: 2
Per Serving
Calories 102

Ingredients:

½ lb. potatoes

1 teaspoon minced garlic

¼ teaspoon pepper

¼ teaspoon turmeric

1-teaspoon olive oil

Directions:

- Peel and cut the potatoes into cubes then place in a steamer.

- Steam the potatoes over medium heat and once it is done, take the cooked potatoes out of the steamer.
- Using a potato masher mash the potato until soft.
- Next, preheat an oven to 350 F then lines a baking sheet with parchment paper. Set aside.
- After that, place the mashed potato together with the remaining ingredients in a food processor then process until combined.
- Shape the mixture using your hands into medium patties then arrange the potato patties on the prepared baking sheet then bake for about 15 minutes until lightly golden.
- Once it is done, remove from the oven and transfer to a serving dish.
- Serve and enjoy warm.

Warm Zucchini Soup

Serving: 2

Nutrition Facts
Servings: 2
Per Serving
Calories 102
Total Fat 2.5g
Saturated Fat 0.4g
Trans Fat 0g
Cholesterol 0mg
Sodium 7mg
Potassium 477mg
Total Carb 18.6g
Dietary Fiber 2.9g
Sugars 1.3g
Protein 2.1g
Nutrition Facts
Servings: 2
Per Serving
Calories 102

Ingredients:

½ cup sliced zucchini

¼ cup diced tomato

¼ cup chopped onion

¼ teaspoon pepper

1 ½ cup vegetables broth

1 tablespoon grated cheddar cheese.

Directions:

- Preheat a pot over medium heat then stir in chopped onion. Sauté the onion until wilted and aromatic.
- Add the zucchini and tomatoes into the pot then pour vegetable broth over the pot.
- Season with pepper then continue to boil.
- Bring to a simmer for approximately 5 minutes then remove from heat.
- Transfer the soup to a serving bowl then sprinkle the grated cheese on top.
- Enjoy warm!

Day 16

Breakfast : Egg Creamy Salads with Avocado
Lunch : Energetic Kale Carrots with Chili
Dinner : Broccoli Quinoa Casserole

Egg Creamy Salad with Avocado

Serving: 2

Nutrition Facts
Servings: 2
Per Serving
Calories 234
Total Fat 17.7g
Saturated Fat 4g
Trans Fat 0g
Cholesterol 328mg
Sodium 132mg
Potassium 451mg
Total Carb 7.7g
Dietary Fiber 4.5g
Sugars 1.8g
Protein 13.1g
Nutrition Facts
Servings: 2
Per Serving
Calories 234

Ingredients:

    4 organic eggs

½ cup mashed avocado

¼ cup chopped onion

4 tablespoons Greek yogurt

1 teaspoon lemon juice

½ teaspoon oregano

¼ teaspoon pepper

Directions:

- Place the eggs in a pot then pour water to cover.
- Bring to boil then once it is boiled, reduce the heat and cook the eggs until completely set.
- Discard the hot water soak the eggs in cold water for a few minutes.
- Peel the boiled eggs then cut into small cubes.
- Add avocado into the eggs then stir in chopped onion and pour yogurt into it. Mix well.
- Splash lemon juice over the salad and sprinkle oregano and pepper on top.
- Serve and enjoy immediately.

Energetic Kale Carrots with Chili

Serving: 2

Nutrition Facts
Servings: 1
Per Serving
Calories 99
Total Fat 2.3g
Saturated Fat 0.3g
Trans Fat 0g
Cholesterol 0mg
Sodium 83mg
Potassium 703mg
Total Carb 17.6g
Dietary Fiber 2.9g
Sugars 2.7g
Protein 3.7g
Nutrition Facts
Servings: 1
Per Serving
Calories 99

Ingredients:

1 ½ cups fresh chopped kale

½ cup shredded carrots

½ teaspoon olive oil

3 teaspoons sliced shallot

2 teaspoon red chili flakes

2 tablespoons water

Directions:

- Preheat a skillet over medium heat then pours olive oil into it.

- When the oil is hot, stir in sliced shallot and chili then sauté until aromatic.
- Next, add shredded carrots into the skillet then pour water into it.
- Stir well until the carrot is tender enough but still crispy.
- After that, add chopped kale into the skillet then cook until soft.
- Transfer the kale and carrots to a serving dish. Enjoy!

30 Day Mediterranean Diet Challenge

Broccoli Quinoa Casserole

Serving: 5

Nutrition Facts
Servings: 5
Per Serving
Calories 175
Total Fat 6.3g
Saturated Fat 2g
Trans Fat 0g
Cholesterol 8mg
Sodium 55mg
Potassium 265mg
Total Carb 23.8g
Dietary Fiber 2.9g
Sugars 2g
Protein 9.7g
Nutrition Facts
Servings: 5
Per Serving
Calories 175

Ingredients:

½ cup cooked quinoa

1-cup broccoli florets

½ teaspoon olive oil

2 tablespoons whole wheat bread crumbs

1-tablespoon whole-wheat flour

½ cup grated cheese

2 tablespoons Greek yogurt

Directions:

- Preheat an oven to 350 F then coat a casserole dish with cooking spray. Set aside.
- Combine all ingredients except cheese in a bowl.
- Using a wooden spatula, mix until combined then transfers to the prepared casserole dish. Spread evenly.
- Sprinkle grated cheese on top then bakes for about 7 minutes or until the cheese is melted.
- Once it is done, remove from the oven and let it cool for a few minutes.
- Serve and enjoy warm.

Day 17

Breakfast : Apple Coconut Oatmeal
Lunch : Orange Green Salads
Dinner : Chicken in Curry Gravy

Apple Coconut Oatmeal

Serving: 1

Nutrition Facts
Servings: 2
Per Serving
Calories 189
Total Fat 9.4g
Saturated Fat 7.3g
Trans Fat 0g
Cholesterol 0mg
Sodium 9mg
Potassium 232mg
Total Carb 24g
Dietary Fiber 4.4g
Sugars 7.4g
Protein 4.3g
Nutrition Facts
Servings: 2
Per Serving
Calories 189

Ingredients:

¼ cup coconut milk

¾ cup water

½ cup chopped apple

¼ teaspoon pepper

½ cup oats

3 tablespoons Greek yogurt

1-tablespoon coconut flakes

Directions:

- Place sliced apple in a saucepan then pours coconut milk into the pan.
- Season with pepper then bring to boil over medium heat.
- Once it is boiled, add oats into the pan and stir for about 5 minutes until the oats are completely cooked.
- Turn the heat off then stirs in yogurt into the pan.
- Transfer the cooked oats to a bowl and sprinkle coconut flakes on top.
- Serve and enjoy immediately.

Orange Green Salads

Serving: 2

Nutrition Facts
Servings: 2
Per Serving
Calories 241
Total Fat 19.8g
Saturated Fat 4.1g
Trans Fat 0g
Cholesterol 0mg
Sodium 50mg
Potassium 761mg
Total Carb 20.4g
Dietary Fiber 10.7g
Sugars 3.5g
Protein 3.1g
Nutrition Facts
Servings: 2
Per Serving
Calories 241

Ingredients:

- 1 ripe avocado
- 2 medium carrots
- 1 lemon

Directions:

- Peel the carrot the place in a steamer over medium heat.
- Steam the carrots for about 2 minutes or until the carrots are tender enough but still crispy.
- Remove the steamed carrots from the steamer then cut into medium cubes.

- Place the chopped carrot in a bowl then add avocado flesh into the bowl.
- Cut lemon into halves then squeeze the juice over the salads. Mix well.
- Serve and enjoy right away.

30 Day Mediterranean Diet Challenge

Chicken in Curry Gravy

Serving: 4

Nutrition Facts
Servings: 4
Per Serving
Calories 262
Total Fat 12.4g
Saturated Fat 7.6g
Trans Fat 0g
Cholesterol 87mg
Sodium 79mg
Potassium 317mg
Total Carb 3g
Dietary Fiber 1g
Sugars 1g
Protein 33.8g
Nutrition Facts
Servings: 4
Per Serving
Calories 262

Ingredients:

½ tablespoon olive oil

2 teaspoon minced garlic

2 teaspoon sliced shallots

1-teaspoon curry

½ teaspoon ginger

½ teaspoon pepper

1 lb. chopped chicken

2 cups water

½ cups coconut milk

Directions:

- Preheat a skillet over medium heat then pour olive oil into it.
- Once it is hot, stir in minced garlic and sliced shallot then sauté until lightly brown and aromatic.
- Add chopped chicken into the skillet then season with curry, ginger, and pepper. Using a wooden spatula, stir the chicken until completely seasoned.
- Pour water over chicken then bring to boil.
- Once it is boiled, reduce the heat and continue to cook for about 15 minutes or until the chicken is tender.
- After that, pour the coconut milk then bring to a simmer while stirring occasionally.
- Once it is done, remove from heat and transfer the chicken curry to a serving bowl.
- Serve and enjoy warm.

30 Day Mediterranean Diet Challenge

Day 18

Breakfast : Turkey Sandwich in Garlic
Lunch : Cheesy Spinach Mushroom
Dinner : Spicy Eggplant Stew

Turkey Sandwich in Garlic

Serving: 1

Nutrition Facts
Servings: 1
Per Serving
Calories 259
Total Fat 5.7g
Saturated Fat 0.9g
Trans Fat 0g
Cholesterol 18mg
Sodium 269mg
Potassium 130mg
Total Carb 34.2g
Dietary Fiber 10.4g
Sugars 6.3g
Protein 15.2g
Nutrition Facts
Servings: 1
Per Serving
Calories 259

Ingredients:

2 slices whole-grain bread

2 lettuce leaves

1-teaspoon olive oil

2 tablespoons minced garlic

¼ sliced turkey

¼ teaspoon pepper

Directions:

- Preheat a saucepan over medium heat then pour olive oil into it.
- Once it is hot, stir in chopped garlic then sautés until aromatic.
- Next, add sliced turkey into the saucepan then season with pepper. Sauté until the turkey is completely cooked and soft. Set aside.
- Place a slice of bread on a platter then arrange cooked turkey on it.
- Add lettuce leaves after the turkey then cover the sandwich with the remaining bread.
- Serve and enjoy!

Cheesy Spinach Mushroom

Serving: 4

Nutrition Facts
Servings: 2
Per Serving
Calories 104
Total Fat 9.5g
Saturated Fat 2.5g
Trans Fat 0g
Cholesterol 7mg
Sodium 59mg
Potassium 243mg
Total Carb 2.6g
Dietary Fiber 0.8g
Sugars 0.9g
Protein 3.7g
Nutrition Facts
Servings: 2
Per Serving
Calories 104

Ingredients:

- 4 large mushrooms
- 1 cup chopped spinach
- 1-tablespoon olive oil
- 1 teaspoon minced garlic
- 2 tablespoons grated cheese

Directions:

- Preheat an oven to 350 F then lines a baking sheet with parchment paper.
- Place the mushrooms on the prepared baking sheet then set aside.

- Preheat a skillet then pour olive oil into it.
- When it is hot, stir in minced garlic then sautés until aromatic and lightly brown.
- Add chopped spinach together with grated cheese into the skillet then stir gently until completely wilted.
- Put a scoop of cooked spinach on each mushroom then bake for about 15 minutes until the cheese is melted.
- When it is done, remove them from the oven and arrange on a serving platter.
- Serve and enjoy!

Spicy Eggplant Stew

Serving: 2

Nutrition Facts
Servings: 1
Per Serving
Calories 174
Total Fat 14.6g
Saturated Fat 2.2g
Trans Fat 0g
Cholesterol 0mg
Sodium 27mg
Potassium 376mg
Total Carb 11.9g
Dietary Fiber 5.2g
Sugars 6.2g
Protein 1.8g
Nutrition Facts
Servings: 1
Per Serving
Calories 174

Ingredients:

2 tablespoons chopped onion

¼ teaspoon pepper

1-cup water

1 cup chopped eggplant

2 tablespoon chopped red chili

½ cup cubed carrot

1-tablespoon olive oil

1 tablespoon lemon juice

Directions:

- Preheat a pan over medium heat then pour olive oil into the pot.
- Once it is hot, stir in chopped onion and red chilies then sautés until wilted and aromatic.
- Pour water into the pan then bring to boil.
- When it is boiled, add chopped eggplant together with cubed carrot.
- Splash lemon juice over the vegetables then brings to a simmer for approximately 15 minutes.
- Transfer the eggplant stew into a serving bowl then serve hot.

Day 19

Breakfast : Cheesy Asparagus Frittata
Lunch : Tamarind Cabbage Stew
Dinner : Shrimps Satay Sweet Honey

Cheesy Asparagus Frittata

Serving: 1

Nutrition Facts
Servings: 1
Per Serving
Calories 191
Total Fat 12g
Saturated Fat 3.8g
Trans Fat 0g
Cholesterol 333mg
Sodium 315mg
Potassium 290mg
Total Carb 7.4g
Dietary Fiber 2g
Sugars 4.7g
Protein 14.9g
Nutrition Facts
Servings: 1
Per Serving
Calories 191

Ingredients:

2 organic eggs

2 tablespoons olive

4 tablespoons fresh milk

½ cup chopped asparagus

3 tablespoons feta crumbles

Directions:

- Preheat an oven to 350 F then coats a small casserole dish with cooking spray.
- Crack the eggs then place in a bowl. Using a whisker, whisk the eggs until fluffy.
- Add the remaining ingredients into the bowl then stir until combined.
- Pour the egg mixture into the coated casserole dish then spread evenly.
- Bake for about 15 minutes until the egg is set.
- Once it is done, remove from the oven and let it cool for a few minutes
- Serve and enjoy warm.

Tamarind Cabbage Stew

Serving: 2

Nutrition Facts
Servings: 1
Per Serving
Calories 174
Total Fat 14.6g
Saturated Fat 2.2g
Trans Fat 0g
Cholesterol 0mg
Sodium 27mg
Potassium 376mg
Total Carb 11.9g
Dietary Fiber 5.2g
Sugars 6.2g
Protein 1.8g
Nutrition Facts
Servings: 1
Per Serving
Calories 174

Ingredients:

1 cup chopped cabbage

½ cup chopped carrot

2 tablespoons corn kernels

2 cups water

1 teaspoon sliced garlic

1 teaspoon sliced shallot

1 bay leaf

½ teaspoon tamarind

Directions:

- Place chopped cabbage and carrots in a pot.
- Add bay leaf, garlic, shallot, and tamarind into the pot then pour water over the ingredients.
- Bring to boil over medium heat and once it is done, reduce the heat and continue cooking for about 6 minutes or until the vegetables are tender enough.
- Transfer the stew to a serving bowl then enjoy warm.

Shrimps Satay Sweet Honey

Serving: 1

Nutrition Facts
Servings: 2
Per Serving
Calories 136
Total Fat 7.6g
Saturated Fat 1g
Trans Fat 0g
Cholesterol 83mg
Sodium 96mg
Potassium 20mg
Total Carb 9.6g
Dietary Fiber 0.2g
Sugars 8.7g
Protein 9.2g
Nutrition Facts
Servings: 2
Per Serving
Calories 136

Ingredients:

- 3 teaspoons olive oil
- 1 teaspoon minced garlic
- ½ teaspoon ginger
- ¼ teaspoon pepper
- 1-tablespoon honey
- 1-cup fresh medium shrimps

Directions:

- Combine minced garlic, ginger, and pepper in a bowl then mix until incorporated.
- Add the shrimps into the bowl then rub with the spices mixture. Let it sit for about 10 minutes.
- Preheat an oven to 400 F then coats a baking sheet with cooking spray. Set aside.
- Place olive oil and honey in a flat platter then mix until incorporated.
- Prick the spiced shrimps with wooden skewers then brush them with honey sauce mixture.
- Arrange the spiced fish satay on the prepared baking sheet then bake for about 15 minutes until tender.
- Removes from the oven then transfer to a serving platter.
- Sprinkle sliced shallots and red chilies over the satay then enjoy warm.

Day 20

Breakfast : Red Apple Pancake
Lunch : Avocado Salads with Chicken and Mushroom
Dinner : Quinoa Chickpea Curry

Red Apple Pancake

Serving: 6

Nutrition Facts
Servings: 6
Per Serving
Calories 140
Total Fat 1.3g
Saturated Fat 0.2g
Trans Fat 0g
Cholesterol 0mg
Sodium 22mg
Potassium 155mg
Total Carb 29.1g
Dietary Fiber 2.8g
Sugars 9.5g
Protein 3.7g
Nutrition Facts
Servings: 6
Per Serving
Calories 140

Ingredients:

1-½ cups whole-wheat flour

1-½ cups soymilk

2 fresh red apples

1 tablespoon lemon juice

1-teaspoon cinnamon

¼ teaspoon olive oil

Directions:

- Discard the apple's seeds then cut into slices.
- Drizzle lemon juice over the apples then set aside.
- Place the whole-wheat flour and cinnamon in a bowl then make a hole in the center of the bowl.
- Pour soymilk into the hole then using a whisker, combine the ingredients until smooth.
- Preheat a frying pan over medium heat the brush olive oil over the surface.
- Once it is hot, pour about ¼ cup of the batter on the hot pan.
- Sprinkle sliced apples on top then cooks for about a minute.
- Flip the pancake and continue to cook the pancake until the pancake is completely cooked and both sides are lightly brown.
- Remove the pancake from the pan then repeats with the remaining batter.
- Arrange the apple pancakes on a serving platter then serve right away.

Avocado Salads with Chicken and Mushroom

Serving: 4

Nutrition Facts
Servings: 8
Per Serving
Calories 237
Total Fat 12.2g
Saturated Fat 2.7g
Trans Fat 0g
Cholesterol 1mg
Sodium 75mg
Potassium 562mg
Total Carb 25.4g
Dietary Fiber 8.9g
Sugars 6.9g
Protein 9g
Nutrition Facts
Servings: 8
Per Serving
Calories 237

Ingredients:

1 ripe avocado

½ cup chopped mushroom

½ cup chopped chicken breast

2 tablespoons chopped onion

1 teaspoon minced garlic

½ teaspoon ginger

1-cup water

½ teaspoon olive oil

¼ teaspoon pepper

Directions:

- First, cook the chicken and mushroom.
- Preheat a pan over medium heat then pour olive oil into it.
- Once it is hot, stir in chopped onion and minced garlic into the pan then sauté until wilted and aromatic.
- Next, add the tuna and chopped chicken then season with ginger. Stir well.
- After that, pour water into the pan and bring to boil.
- Once it is boiled, reduce the heat and cook until the water is completely absorbed into the chicken and mushroom
- Sprinkle pepper over the salads then using two forks mix until combined.
- Serves immediately.

30 Day Mediterranean Diet Challenge

Quinoa Chickpea Curry

Serving: 8

Nutrition Facts
Servings: 8
Per Serving
Calories 281
Total Fat 13.7g
Saturated Fat 7.2g
Trans Fat 0g
Cholesterol 0mg
Sodium 14mg
Potassium 521mg
Total Carb 33g
Dietary Fiber 7.2g
Sugars 4.5g
Protein 8.9g
Nutrition Facts
Servings: 8
Per Serving
Calories 281

Ingredients:

1 cup cooked quinoa

1-cup coconut milk

1 cup diced tomatoes

2 tablespoons turmeric powder

2 tablespoons olive oil

¼ cup chopped onion

1 teaspoon minced garlic

1 cup cooked chickpeas

1 tablespoon chopped leek

Directions:

- Place the cooked quinoa in a saucepan then add diced tomatoes and turmeric powder into it.
- Pour coconut milk over the quinoa then bring to boil while stirring occasionally.
- Once it is boiled, reduce the heat and bring to a simmer for about 15 minutes. Set aside.
- Preheat a frying pan over medium heat then pour olive oil into it.
- Once it is hot, stir in chopped onion and minced garlic then sautés until wilted and aromatic.
- Add the chickpeas and cook for about 4 minutes.
- After that, stir in the cooked quinoa into the pan and stir vigorously until the mixture is completely combined.
- Once is done, transfer to a serving dish and sprinkle chopped leek on top.
- Serve and enjoy.

Day 21

Breakfast : Cinnamon Simple Oatmeal
Lunch : Sautéed Green Spinach
Dinner : Warm Lamb Skewers

Cinnamon Simple Oatmeal

Serving: 4

Nutrition Facts
Servings: 3
Per Serving
Calories 104
Total Fat 3.8g
Saturated Fat 0.6g
Trans Fat 0g
Cholesterol 5mg
Sodium 45mg
Potassium 139mg
Total Carb 9.3g
Dietary Fiber 1.2g
Sugars 3.3g
Protein 9.2g
Nutrition Facts
Servings: 3
Per Serving
Calories 104

Ingredients:

¼ cup oats

1 cup Greek yogurt

2 tablespoons mixed nuts

½ teaspoon cinnamon

Directions:

- Pour Greek yogurt into a bowl then stir in oats.
- Using a spoon, mix the ingredients until combined.
- Sprinkle mixed nuts over the oats then dust cinnamon on top.
- Serve and enjoy immediately.

Sautéed Green Spinach

Serving: 1

Nutrition Facts
Servings: 1
Per Serving
Calories 66
Total Fat 2.7g
Saturated Fat 0.4g
Trans Fat 0g
Cholesterol 0mg
Sodium 32mg
Potassium 335mg
Total Carb 9.5g
Dietary Fiber 2.8g
Sugars 1.6g
Protein 3.2g
Nutrition Facts
Servings: 1
Per Serving
Calories 66

Ingredients:

1-cup fresh chopped spinach

½ teaspoon olive oil

3 teaspoons sliced garlic

2 tablespoons water

Directions:

- Preheat a skillet over medium heat then pours olive oil into it.
- Once it is hot, stir in sliced garlic then sautés until lightly brown and aromatic.

- Next, add chopped spinach into the skillet then stir well until spinach is tender enough but still crispy.
- Transfer the sautéed spinach to a serving dish. Enjoy!

Warm Lamb Skewers

Serving: 1

Nutrition Facts
Servings: 1
Per Serving
Calories 66
Total Fat 2.7g
Saturated Fat 0.4g
Trans Fat 0g
Cholesterol 0mg
Sodium 32mg
Potassium 335mg
Total Carb 9.5g
Dietary Fiber 2.8g
Sugars 1.6g
Protein 3.2g
Nutrition Facts
Servings: 1
Per Serving
Calories 66

Ingredients:

1 teaspoon minced garlic

½ teaspoon ginger

1-tablespoon soy sauce

½ teaspoon coriander

1 lb. lamb chunks

¼ teaspoon pepper

Directions:

- Place garlic in a plate together with ginger, soy sauce, and coriander. Stir until incorporated

- Rub the lamb chunks with the spicy mixture then let it sit for about 30 minutes until the spices are completely absorbed.
- After 30 minutes, prick the lamb using wooden skewers then place on a plate.
- Next, preheat a grill over medium heat.
- Once the grill is hot, carefully grill the lamb until it completely cooked.
- Serve and enjoy warm.

Day 22

Breakfast : Nutritious Veggie Sandwich
Lunch : Spicy Tropical Salads
Dinner : Original Baked Chicken Wings

Nutritious Veggie Sandwich

Serving: 2

Nutrition Facts
Servings: 2
Per Serving
Calories 175
Total Fat 4.9g
Saturated Fat 1.3g
Trans Fat 0g
Cholesterol 0mg
Sodium 316mg
Potassium 143mg
Total Carb 29.4g

30 Day Mediterranean Diet Challenge

Dietary Fiber 3g
Sugars 2.9g
Protein 5.6g
Nutrition Facts
Servings: 2
Per Serving
Calories 175

Ingredients:

- 3 slices whole-grain bread
- ½ cup sliced tomatoes
- 1-teaspoon olive oil
- 2 tablespoons chopped onion
- 1 tablespoon shredded carrot
- 2 tablespoons shredded cabbage
- ¼ teaspoon pepper

Directions:

- Preheat a saucepan over medium heat then pour olive oil into it.
- Once it is hot, stir in chopped onion then sautés until aromatic.
- Next, add carrot and cabbage into the saucepan then season with pepper. Sauté until the vegetable are wilted and tender. Set aside.
- Place a slice of bread on a platter then arranges tomatoes on it.
- Place another slice of bread after tomatoes then add the sautéed vegetable on it.
- Cover the sandwich with the remaining bread and serve.

Spicy Tropical Salads

Serving: 2

Nutrition Facts
Servings: 2
Per Serving
Calories 188
Total Fat 1.1g
Saturated Fat 0.2g
Trans Fat 0g
Cholesterol 0mg
Sodium 11mg
Potassium 655mg
Total Carb 47.5g
Dietary Fiber 6.4g
Sugars 38.3g
Protein 2.9g
Nutrition Facts
Servings: 2
Per Serving
Calories 188

Ingredients:

1 large apple

1 unripe mango

1 medium cucumber

1-teaspoon tamarind

5 red chilies

1-cup water

Directions:

- Chop the apple, mango, and cucumber then place in a bowl. Set aside.

- Place tamarind, red chilies, and water in a blender then blend until incorporated.
- Pour the liquid mixture over the fruits then cover with plastic wrap.
- Chill the fruits in the refrigerator for at least an hour until the liquid is completely absorbed.
- Enjoy it at lunch.

Original Baked Chicken Wings

Serving: 5

Nutrition Facts
Servings: 2
Per Serving
Calories 136
Total Fat 7.6g
Saturated Fat 1g
Trans Fat 0g
Cholesterol 83mg
Sodium 96mg
Potassium 20mg
Total Carb 9.6g
Dietary Fiber 0.2g
Sugars 8.7g
Protein 9.2g
Nutrition Facts
Servings: 2
Per Serving
Calories 136

Ingredients:

½ tablespoon olive oil

2 teaspoon minced garlic

½ teaspoon pepper

1 lb. chicken wings

Directions:

- Combine minced garlic and pepper in a bowl then mix until incorporated.
- Add the chicken wings into the bowl then rub with the spices mixture. Let it sit for about an hour.

- Preheat an oven to 400 F then coats a baking sheet with cooking spray. Set aside.
- Arrange the spiced chicken wings on the prepared baking sheet then bake for about 25 minutes until tender.
- Removes from the oven then transfer to a serving platter.
- Serve and enjoy warm.

Day 23

Breakfast : Healthy Baked Beans on Toast
Lunch : Avocado Lentils Salads
Dinner : Special Curry Pasta

Healthy Baked Beans on Toast

Serving: 3

Nutrition Facts
Servings: 3
Per Serving
Calories 115
Total Fat 2g
Saturated Fat 0.4g
Trans Fat 0.2g
Cholesterol 0mg
Sodium 413mg
Potassium 332mg
Total Carb 19.5g
Dietary Fiber 4.5g
Sugars 5.4g
Protein 5.7g
Nutrition Facts
Servings: 3
Per Serving
Calories 115

Ingredients:

½ teaspoon olive oil

½ cup chopped onion

1 teaspoon minced garlic

¼ cup vegetable broth

1-½ cups cooked beans

½ cup tomato sauce

¼ teaspoon pepper

½ teaspoon chopped celeries

3 slices whole-wheat bread

Directions:

- Preheat olive oil in a skillet over medium heat.
- Stir in chopped onion and minced garlic into the skillet then sautés until wilted and aromatic.
- Pour vegetable broth into the skillet and after that add the baked beans into the skillet.
- Season with pepper and cook for a few minutes until the liquid is completely absorbed into the baked beans.
- Next, stir in tomato sauce into the beans and stir well.
- Sprinkle chopped celeries over the beans then remove from heat.
- Toast the whole-wheat bread until golden.
- Once it is done, places the whole-wheat bread on a serving platter then drop two scoops of baked beans on each slice. Spread evenly.
- Serve and enjoy warm.

Avocado Lentils Salads

Serving: 4

Nutrition Facts
Servings: 4
Per Serving
Calories 198
Total Fat 10.8g
Saturated Fat 1.8g
Trans Fat 0g
Cholesterol 0mg
Sodium 6mg
Potassium 322mg
Total Carb 20.3g
Dietary Fiber 8.6g
Sugars 4.9g
Protein 6.6g
Nutrition Facts
Servings: 4
Per Serving
Calories 198

Ingredients:

½ cup lentils

2 cups water

1-tablespoon honey

2 tablespoons olive oil

½ cup chopped avocado

Directions:

- Place lentils in a saucepan then pour water to cover the lentils.
- Bring to boil over medium heat and once it is boiled, reduce the heat and bring to a

simmer uncover for approximately 20 minutes or until the lentils are tender.
- Strain the lentils then pour olive oil and honey over the lentils.
- Remove the pan from the heat then stirs in chopped avocado into the saucepan.
- Transfer the lentils to a serving dish then enjoy!

Special Curry Pasta

Serving: 2

Nutrition Facts
Servings: 2
Per Serving
Calories 142
Total Fat 9.5g
Saturated Fat 6.7g
Trans Fat 0g
Cholesterol 10mg
Sodium 17mg
Potassium 264mg
Total Carb 13.1g
Dietary Fiber 1.9g
Sugars 2.7g
Protein 3g
Nutrition Facts
Servings: 2
Per Serving
Calories 142

Ingredients:

1 oz. uncooked penne pasta

3 tablespoons red chili flakes

2 tablespoons chopped celery

2 tablespoons chopped onion

½ cup cherry tomatoes

1-teaspoon curry powder

¼ cup coconut milk

¼ tablespoon olive oil

¼ teaspoon pepper

Directions:

- Cook the pasta according to the package direction. Drain then place on a serving dish.
- Meanwhile, preheat a skillet over medium heat then pour olive oil into it.
- When the oil is hot, stir in chopped onion and chili flakes then sauté until wilted and aromatic.
- Pour coconut milk and add curry powder into the skillet then bring to boil.
- Add cherry tomatoes into the skillet then cook until the tomatoes are broken down.
- Season with pepper then cook for about 2 minutes.
- Add the cooked spaghetti into the skillet then gently stir it until well mixed.
- Transfer the pasta to a serving dish then garnish with chopped celery.
- Enjoy immediately.

Day 24

Breakfast : Baked Sweet Potato with Cinnamon
Lunch : Special Raw Fruits
Dinner : Chicken Tomato Soup

Baked Sweet Potato with Cinnamon

Serving: 3

Nutrition Facts
Servings: 3
Per Serving
Calories 140
Total Fat 2.5g
Saturated Fat 0.4g
Trans Fat 0g
Cholesterol 0mg
Sodium 9mg
Potassium 819mg
Total Carb 28.5g
Dietary Fiber 4.5g
Sugars 0.5g
Protein 1.6g
Nutrition Facts
Servings: 3
Per Serving
Calories 140

Ingredients:

1 ½ teaspoon olive oil

2 medium sweet potatoes

1-teaspoon cinnamon

Directions:

- Preheat an oven to 350 F then lines a baking sheet with parchment paper. Set aside.
- Cut the sweet potatoes into thick slices then arrange them on the prepared baking sheet.
- Splash olive oil over the sweet potatoes and bake for about 45 minutes until the sweet potatoes are tender.
- Sprinkle cinnamon on top then re-bake for approximately 3 minutes.
- Remove the baked sweet potatoes from the oven then transfer to a platter.
- Serve and enjoy warm.

Special Raw Fruits

Serving: 1

Nutrition Facts
Servings: 2
Per Serving
Calories 234
Total Fat 19.7g
Saturated Fat 4.2g
Trans Fat 0g
Cholesterol 0mg
Sodium 22mg
Potassium 701mg
Total Carb 14.9g
Dietary Fiber 7.4g
Sugars 2.8g
Protein 3.2g
Nutrition Facts
Servings: 2
Per Serving
Calories 234

Ingredients:

½ cup watermelon cubes

1 ripe avocado

1 cup chopped kale

1 tablespoon lemon juice

Directions:

- Peel and cut the avocado flesh into cubes then place in a bowl.
- Add watermelon cubes and chopped kale into the same bowl then using two forks mix until combined.

- Splash lemon juice over the salads then chill in the refrigerator for at least two hours.
- Serve and enjoy immediately.

Chicken Tomato Soup

Serving: 4

Nutrition Facts
Servings: 4
Per Serving
Calories 150
Total Fat 4.5g
Saturated Fat 0.9g
Trans Fat 0g
Cholesterol 28mg
Sodium 414mg
Potassium 311mg
Total Carb 10g
Dietary Fiber 0.9g
Sugars 1.6g
Protein 16.2g
Nutrition Facts
Servings: 4
Per Serving
Calories 150

Ingredients:

2 cups chicken broth

1 ½ cup chopped chicken breast

½ cup corn kernels

½ cup mashed tomato

½ cup diced tomato

1 teaspoon minced garlic

1 bay leaf

½ teaspoon pepper

¼ teaspoon olive oil

Directions:

- Preheat a soup pot over medium heat and pour olive oil into it.
- Stir in minced garlic then sautés until wilted and aromatic.
- Add chopped chicken and corn kernels into the pot and stir for a few minutes.
- Pour chicken broth together with mashed tomato and diced tomato into the pot then bring to boil.
- Once it is boiled, season with bay leaf and pepper.
- Bring to a simmer for approximately 5 minutes then transfer to a serving bowl.
- Serve and enjoy hot.

Day 25

Breakfast : Sweet Apple Frittata
Lunch   : Hot Salmon Cakes
Dinner   : Tasty Lentils Soup

Sweet Apple Frittata

Serving: 5

Nutrition Facts
Servings: 5
Per Serving
Calories 196
Total Fat 8.9g
Saturated Fat 2.7g
Trans Fat 0g
Cholesterol 330mg
Sodium 140mg
Potassium 261mg
Total Carb 14.8g
Dietary Fiber 2.2g
Sugars 11.8g
Protein 15.7g
Nutrition Facts
Servings: 5
Per Serving
Calories 196

Ingredients:

10 organic eggs

1 cup Greek yogurt

2 fresh green apples

Directions:

- Peel and discard the apple seeds then cut into thinly slices. Set aside.
- Preheat an oven to 350 F then coats a medium baking dish with cooking spray.
- Crack the eggs then place in a bowl. Using a whisker, whisk the eggs until fluffy.
- Add yogurt into the bowl then stir until combined.
- Pour the egg mixture into the prepared baking dish then spread evenly.
- Arrange the apples on the top then bakes for about 15 minutes until the egg is set.
- Once it is done, remove from the oven and let it cool for a few minutes.
- Serve and enjoy.

Hot Salmon Cakes

Serving: 4

Nutrition Facts
Servings: 4
Per Serving
Calories 162
Total Fat 8.2g
Saturated Fat 1.2g
Trans Fat 0g
Cholesterol 50mg
Sodium 50mg
Potassium 441mg
Total Carb 0.4g
Dietary Fiber 0.1g
Sugars 0g
Protein 22.1g
Nutrition Facts
Servings: 4
Per Serving
Calories 162

Ingredients:

1 lb. salmon fillet

1 teaspoon minced garlic

¼ teaspoon pepper

2 tablespoons red chili flakes

¼ teaspoon ginger

1-teaspoon olive oil

Directions:

- Preheat an oven to 400 F then coats a baking sheet with cooking oil. Set aside.

- Place all of the ingredients in a food processor then process until combined.
- Shape the mixture using your hands into medium patties and place them on the prepared baking sheet.
- Bake for about 15 minutes until lightly golden then remove from the oven.
- Once it is done, remove from the oven and transfer to a serving dish.
- Serve and enjoy warm.

Tasty Lentils Soup

Serving: 5

Nutrition Facts
Servings: 5
Per Serving
Calories 167
Total Fat 1.5g
Saturated Fat 0.3g
Trans Fat 0g
Cholesterol 0mg
Sodium 471mg
Potassium 524mg
Total Carb 26.8g
Dietary Fiber 12.6g
Sugars 2.5g
Protein 11.9g
Nutrition Facts
Servings: 5
Per Serving
Calories 167

Ingredients:

½ teaspoon olive oil

1 cup chopped onion

½ teaspoon turmeric

½ teaspoon cumin

½ teaspoon chili

¼ teaspoon pepper

1 teaspoon minced garlic

1-¾ cups water

1 cup lentils

¼ cup chopped cilantro

1 ½ cups vegetable broth

½ cup diced tomato

Directions:

- Preheat a Dutch oven over medium heat then pour olive oil into it.
- Once it is hot, stir in onion and minced garlic then sauté until wilted and aromatic.
- Add turmeric, cumin, chili, and pepper into the Dutch oven then pour water into it. Bring to boil.
- Once it is boiled, stir in lentils then reduce the heat and bring to a simmer for about an hour.
- Remove the soup from heat then transfer to a blender and blend until smooth.
- Pour the smooth lentils soup to a serving bowl then serve immediately.

Day 26

Breakfast : Savory Oatmeal Breakfast
Lunch : Vegetable Tortilla Roll
Dinner : Mushroom Kabobs Black Pepper

Savory Oatmeal Breakfast

Serving: 1

Nutrition Facts
Servings: 1
Per Serving
Calories 237
Total Fat 4.3g
Saturated Fat 0.9g
Trans Fat 0g
Cholesterol 3mg
Sodium 786mg
Potassium 629mg
Total Carb 34.9g
Dietary Fiber 5.5g
Sugars 5.4g
Protein 15.3g
Nutrition Facts
Servings: 1
Per Serving
Calories 237

Ingredients:

1-cup vegetable broth

½ cup chopped tomatoes

¼ teaspoon pepper

½ cup oats

3 tablespoons Greek yogurt

1 tablespoon chopped leek

Directions:

- Place chopped tomatoes in a saucepan then pours vegetable broth into the pan.
- Season with pepper then bring to boil over medium heat.
- Once it is boiled, add oats into the pan and stir for about 5 minutes until the oats are completely cooked.
- Turn the heat off then stirs in yogurt into the pan.
- Transfer the cooked oats to a bowl and sprinkle chopped leek on top.
- Serve and enjoy immediately.

30 Day Mediterranean Diet Challenge

Vegetable Tortilla Roll

Serving: 2

Nutrition Facts
Servings: 2
Per Serving
Calories 106
Total Fat 1.8g
Saturated Fat 0.3g
Trans Fat 0g
Cholesterol 0mg
Sodium 28mg
Potassium 252mg
Total Carb 21.5g
Dietary Fiber 3.4g
Sugars 3g
Protein 3g
Nutrition Facts
Servings: 2
Per Serving
Calories 106

Ingredients:

- 2 whole-wheat tortillas
- 1 cup chopped lettuce
- ½ cup corn kernels
- ¼ cup diced carrots
- ¼ cup chopped onion
- ¼ teaspoon olive oil

Directions:

- Preheat a skillet over medium heat then pours olive oil into it.

- Once it is hot, stir in chopped onion then sautés until wilted and aromatic.
- Add corn kernels and diced carrots then sauté until wilted and cooked through.
- Remove from heat then stir in chopped lettuce. Mix well.
- Place the tortillas on a flat surface then brush with water.
- Divide the vegetable mixture into two tortillas then tightly roll them.
- Using a sharp knife, cut the tortillas then arranges on a serving platter.
- Serve and enjoy immediately.

Mushroom Kabobs Black Pepper

Serving: 1

Nutrition Facts
Servings: 1
Per Serving
Calories 143
Total Fat 14.3g
Saturated Fat 2g
Trans Fat 0g
Cholesterol 0mg
Sodium 7mg
Potassium 268mg
Total Carb 4.2g
Dietary Fiber 1.2g
Sugars 1.3g
Protein 2.6g
Nutrition Facts
Servings: 1
Per Serving
Calories 143

Ingredients:

- 3 teaspoons olive oil
- 1 teaspoon minced garlic
- ½ teaspoon black pepper
- 1-cup mushroom
- 1 tablespoon chopped parsley

Directions:

- Preheat an oven to 425 F then coats a baking sheet with cooking oil. Set aside.

- Place minced garlic and black pepper in a bowl then pour olive oil into the bowl. Mix until incorporated.
- Add the mushroom into the bowl then rub with the black pepper mixture. Let it sit for about 10 minutes.
- Prick the mushroom with wooden skewers and arrange them on the prepared baking sheet.
- Bake for about 15 minutes until tender then removes from the oven.
- Arrange the mushroom kabobs on a serving platter then enjoy warm.

Day 27

Breakfast : Whole-Wheat Poffertjes with Cinnamon
Lunch : Sautéed Chicken in Wrap
Dinner : Quinoa Bowl with Cucumber and Kale

Whole-Wheat Poffertjes with Cinnamon

Serving: 6

Nutrition Facts

179

Servings: 6
Per Serving
Calories 170
Total Fat 9.9g
Saturated Fat 8.5g
Trans Fat 0g
Cholesterol 0mg
Sodium 6mg
Potassium 129mg
Total Carb 18.4g
Dietary Fiber 1.6g
Sugars 1.4g
Protein 3.1g
Nutrition Facts
Servings: 6
Per Serving
Calories 170

Ingredients:

- 1-½ cups whole-wheat flour
- 1-½ cups almond milk
- 1-teaspoon cinnamon
- ¼ teaspoon olive oil

Directions:

- Place the whole-wheat flour in a bowl then make a hole in the center of the bowl.
- Pour almond milk into the hole then using a whisker, combine the ingredients until smooth.
- Season with cinnamon then mix until combined.
- Preheat a poffertjes pan over medium heat the brush olive oil over the surface.
- Once it is hot, pour about the batter on each hole of the hot pan.
- Cook the poffertjes then flip until becoming balls.

- Continue to cook until the poffertjes is completely cooked and lightly brown.
- Remove the poffertjes from the pan then arrange on a serving platter then serve right away.

Sautéed Chicken in Wrap

Serving: 2

Nutrition Facts
Servings: 2
Per Serving
Calories 176
Total Fat 6.6g
Saturated Fat 1.7g
Trans Fat 0g
Cholesterol 38mg
Sodium 208mg
Potassium 141mg
Total Carb 14.4g
Dietary Fiber 2.5g
Sugars 1.7g
Protein 14.7g
Nutrition Facts
Servings: 2
Per Serving
Calories 176

Ingredients:

1 cup chopped chicken breast

¼ cup chopped celeries

½ teaspoon olive oil

½ teaspoon pepper

1 tablespoon chopped onion

2 whole-grain tortillas

Directions:

- Preheat a skillet over medium heat then pours olive oil into it.

- Once it is hot, stir in chopped onion then sautés until wilted and aromatic.
- Next, add chopped chicken into the skillet then season with pepper. Stir well until the chicken is wilted and completely cooked.
- After that, stir in chopped celery then mix until just combined.
- Place the whole-grain tortillas on a flat surface then put sautéed chicken on each tortilla.
- Roll the tortillas tightly then enjoy at lunch.

Quinoa Bowl with Cucumber and Kale

Serving: 4

Nutrition Facts
Servings: 4
Per Serving
Calories 243
Total Fat 9.9g
Saturated Fat 1.5g
Trans Fat 0g
Cholesterol 2mg
Sodium 24mg
Potassium 400mg
Total Carb 31.9g
Dietary Fiber 3.5g
Sugars 2.1g
Protein 7.7g
Nutrition Facts
Servings: 4
Per Serving
Calories 243

Ingredients:

1 cup cooked quinoa

½ cup low fat milk

2 tablespoons olive oil

¼ cup chopped onion

1 teaspoon minced garlic

1 cup chopped kale

½ cup cucumber cubes

Directions:

- Preheat a skillet over medium heat then pour olive oil into it.
- Once it is hot, stir in chopped onion and minced garlic then sautés until wilted and aromatic.
- Add chopped kale and cucumber cubes into the skillet then sauté until cooked.
- Next, pour low fat milk into the skillet and stir well.
- After that, stir in the cooked quinoa into the skillet and stir vigorously until the mixture is completely combined.
- Once is done, transfer to a serving dish and enjoy.

Day 28

Breakfast : Lemon Scones with Almond
Lunch : Creamy Cheesy Pasta
Dinner : Appetizing Cauliflower Rice

Lemon Scones with Almond

Serving: 4

Nutrition Facts
Servings: 4
Per Serving
Calories 208
Total Fat 8.7g
Saturated Fat 3.8g
Trans Fat 0g
Cholesterol 1mg
Sodium 8mg
Potassium 157mg
Total Carb 26.9g
Dietary Fiber 2g
Sugars 1.5g
Protein 6.6g
Nutrition Facts
Servings: 4
Per Serving
Calories 208

Ingredients:

1-cup whole-wheat flour

2-½ tablespoons almond butter

1 teaspoon lemon zest

1 tablespoon lemon juice

4 tablespoons Greek yogurt

¼ cup almond milk

Directions:

- Preheat an oven to 425 F then lines a baking sheet with parchment paper.
- Combine the whole-wheat flour with lemon zest in a bowl then add sliced almond butter into the bowl.
- Slowly pour Greek yogurt, lemon juice, and almond milk into the bowl then knead until becoming dough.
- Form the dough into small patties then arrange on the prepared baking sheet.
- Bake for approximately 15 minutes or until the scones are lightly golden.
- Remove the scones from the heat then transfer to a serving dish.
- Serve and enjoy.

Creamy Cheesy Pasta

Serving: 2

Nutrition Facts
Servings: 2
Per Serving
Calories 115
Total Fat 4g
Saturated Fat 1.4g
Trans Fat 0g
Cholesterol 17mg
Sodium 54mg
Potassium 82mg
Total Carb 15g
Dietary Fiber 0.4g
Sugars 3.2g
Protein 5.1g
Nutrition Facts
Servings: 2
Per Serving
Calories 115

Ingredients:

1 oz. uncooked penne pasta

¼ cup grated Mozzarella cheese

½ cup fresh milk

1-tablespoon whole-wheat flour

2 tablespoons chopped onion

¼ tablespoon olive oil

¼ teaspoon pepper

Directions:

- Cook the pasta according to the package direction. Drain then place on a serving dish.
- Meanwhile, preheat a skillet over medium heat then pour olive oil into it.
- When the oil is hot, stir in chopped onion then sautés until wilted and aromatic.
- Pour fresh milk and add grated cheese into the skillet then bring to boil.
- Combine whole-wheat flour with water then mix until incorporated.
- Pour the flour mixture into the skillet then cook until creamy.
- Season with pepper then cook for about 2 minutes.
- Pour the cheesy sauce over the cooked pasta then using two forks mix until combined.
- Transfer the pasta to a serving dish then enjoy immediately.

30 Day Mediterranean Diet Challenge

Appetizing Cauliflower Rice

Serving: 2

Nutrition Facts
Servings: 1
Per Serving
Calories 169
Total Fat 14.2g
Saturated Fat 2g
Trans Fat 0g
Cholesterol 0mg
Sodium 930mg
Potassium 365mg
Total Carb 10.3g
Dietary Fiber 3.1g
Sugars 3.7g
Protein 3.1g
Nutrition Facts
Servings: 1
Per Serving
Calories 169

Ingredients:

¾ cup cauliflower florets

3 teaspoons soy sauce

½ teaspoon ginger

¼ teaspoon pepper

3 teaspoons olive oil

1 teaspoon minced garlic

2 tablespoons diced carrots

2 tablespoons chopped onion

Directions:

- Place the cauliflower florets in s food processor then pulse until the cauliflower florets become crumbles.
- Remove from the processor and place in a bowl. Set aside.
- Preheat a skillet over medium heat then pour olive oil into it.
- Once it is hot, stir in garlic and chopped onion then sautés until aromatic and lightly brown.
- Add diced carrot and cauliflower into the skillet then season with ginger and pepper.
- Drizzle soy sauce over the cauliflower then cook for a few minutes while stirring gently.
- When it is done, transfer the cauliflower rice to a serving platter then enjoy warm.

Day 29

Breakfast : Overnight Almond Raisin Oatmeal
Lunch : Refreshing Fruit Bowl
Dinner : Potato White Beans Soup

Overnight Almond Raisin Oatmeal

Serving: 2

Nutrition Facts
Servings: 2
Per Serving
Calories 171
Total Fat 14.7g
Saturated Fat 12.7g
Trans Fat 0g
Cholesterol 0mg
Sodium 10mg
Potassium 210mg
Total Carb 10.4g
Dietary Fiber 2g
Sugars 4.7g
Protein 2.2g
Nutrition Facts
Servings: 2
Per Serving
Calories 171

Ingredients:

2 tablespoons rolled oats

½ cup almond milk

1-tablespoon raisin

Directions:

- Place the oats in a bowl then pour the almond milk into the jar.
- Add raisins into the bowl then mix until combined.
- Cover the bowl with plastic wrap then stores in the refrigerator over night.
- In the next morning, remove the oats from the refrigerator then open the lid.
- Transfer the soaked oats and raisins to a saucepan over medium heat and cook until warm.
- Pour the oats to a serving bowl then serve and enjoy immediately.

Refreshing Fruits Bowl

Serving: 2

Nutrition Facts
Servings: 2
Per Serving
Calories 144
Total Fat 0.8g
Saturated Fat 0.2g
Trans Fat 0g
Cholesterol 0mg
Sodium 4mg
Potassium 431mg
Total Carb 35.9g
Dietary Fiber 4.4g
Sugars 30.2g
Protein 2g
Nutrition Facts
Servings: 2
Per Serving
Calories 144

Ingredients:

½ cup chopped kiwi

½ cup chopped strawberry

½ cup chopped mango

½ cup chopped orange

1 tablespoon lemon juice

1-tablespoon raw honey

Directions:

- Place all of the fruits in a salad bowl then splash lemon juice and drizzle honey on top.

- Carefully stir the fruits until all of the fruits are completely coated with honey and seasoned with lemon juice.
- Cover the salad bowl with plastic wrap then chill in the refrigerator for approximately two hours.
- After two hour, remove from the refrigerator then enjoy cold.

Potato White Beans Soup

Serving: 4

Nutrition Facts
Servings: 4
Per Serving
Calories 184
Total Fat 2g
Saturated Fat 0.3g
Trans Fat 0g
Cholesterol 0mg
Sodium 393mg
Potassium 759mg
Total Carb 28.9g
Dietary Fiber 11.6g
Sugars 1.6g
Protein 13.4g
Nutrition Facts
Servings: 4
Per Serving
Calories 184

Ingredients:

- 2 cups vegetable broth
- ½ cup cubed potato
- ¼ teaspoon olive oil
- 2 tablespoons chopped onion
- 1-cup cooked cannellini beans
- ¼ teaspoon thyme
- 1 teaspoon lemon juice

Directions:

- Preheat a soup pot over medium heat and pour olive oil into it.
- Stir in chopped onion then sautés until wilted and aromatic.
- Pour vegetable broth into the pot then bring to boil.
- Once it is boiled, add potatoes and cannellini beans into the pot then season with thyme, and lemon juice.
- Bring to a simmer for approximately 5 minutes then transfer to a serving bowl.
- Serve and enjoy hot.

30 Day Mediterranean Diet Challenge

Day 30

Breakfast : Thick Omelet in Tomato Gravy
Lunch : Spinach Pizza Tomato
Dinner : Stuffed Tomatoes with Couscous

Thick Omelet in Tomato Gravy

Serving: 1

Nutrition Facts
Servings: 1
Per Serving
Calories 211
Total Fat 16g
Saturated Fat 3.8g
Trans Fat 0g
Cholesterol 327mg
Sodium 136mg
Potassium 369mg
Total Carb 6.4g
Dietary Fiber 1.7g
Sugars 3.9g
Protein 12.1g
Nutrition Facts
Servings: 1
Per Serving
Calories 211

Ingredients:

2 organic eggs

¼ teaspoon pepper

1 ½ teaspoons olive oil

2 tablespoons chopped onion

½ cup diced tomato

1-cup water

Directions:

- Crack the eggs and place in a medium bowl.
- Add pepper and onion into the egg mixture then stir until combined.
- Preheat a non-stick skillet over medium heat then brush with olive oil.
- Once it is hot, pour the egg mixture then cooks for a few minutes until sets.
- Fold the egg and cook again until the egg is completely cooked and lightly brown.
- Remove from the skillet then transfer to a platter.
- Place diced tomato in a blender and pour water into it. Blend until incorporated.
- Strain the tomato mixture then discard the lees.
- Pour the liquid into a saucepan and bring to a simmer.
- Drizzle the gravy over the omelet then serve.

Spinach Pizza Tomato

Serving: 8

Nutrition Facts
Servings: 8
Per Serving
Calories 166
Total Fat 14.1g
Saturated Fat 3g
Trans Fat 0g
Cholesterol 8mg
Sodium 310mg
Potassium 43mg
Total Carb 6g
Dietary Fiber 1.4g
Sugars 2.6g
Protein 4.2g
Nutrition Facts
Servings: 8
Per Serving
Calories 166

Ingredients:

1 whole-wheat pizza crust

1-cup pesto sauce

1-cup halved cherry tomato

1 cup chopped spinach

½ cup olive

¼ cup grated Mozzarella cheese

Directions:

- Preheat an oven to 350 F then coat a pizza pan with cooking spray.
- Drizzle pesto sauce on the pizza crust then spread evenly.
- Place cherry tomatoes, chopped spinach, and olive on the top then cover with grated Mozzarella cheese.
- Bake for approximately 10 minutes or until the cheese is melted.
- Remove from the oven then serve warm.

Stuffed Tomatoes with Couscous

Serving: 8

Nutrition Facts
Servings: 8
Per Serving
Calories 158
Total Fat 4.4g
Saturated Fat 0.7g
Trans Fat 0g
Cholesterol 0mg
Sodium 212mg
Potassium 526mg
Total Carb 24.2g
Dietary Fiber 3.3g
Sugars 5g
Protein 6.4g
Nutrition Facts
Servings: 8
Per Serving
Calories 158

Ingredients:

8 large red tomatoes

1-cup couscous

¼ cup tuna chunks

2 cups vegetable broth

2 tablespoons olive oil

1 teaspoon minced garlic

2 tablespoons chopped parsley

Directions:

- Preheat an oven to 350 F then lines a baking sheet with parchment paper.
- Cut the top of the red tomatoes then gently remove the inside of the tomatoes.
- Place the tomatoes on the prepared baking sheet then set aside.
- Prepare a container with a lid then place couscous in it.
- Pour the vegetable broth into a pot then place on a stove over medium heat.
- Once the vegetable broth is warm, pour over the couscous. Stir well then cover with its lid. Set aside.
- Meanwhile, preheat a skillet then pour olive oil into it.
- When it is hot, stir in minced garlic then sautés until aromatic and lightly brown.
- Add tuna chunks and chopped parsley into the skillet. Gently stir the tuna until it is completely cooked.
- Transfer the cooked tuna to the couscous and mix until combined.
- Fill the tomatoes with couscous and tuna then bake for about 15 minutes.
- When the stuffed tomatoes are done, remove them from the oven and arrange on a serving platter.
- Serve and enjoy!

Made in the USA
Lexington, KY
15 March 2018